I Am Not

By Robert E. Draper

To Ken

CONTENTS

Let us be glad that you will see what you believe,

and that it has been given you to change what you believe.

A Course in Miracles

INTRODUCTION

I, who am neither an I nor a who, like you, who are neither a you nor a who, may have to be in this world for the moment, but that does not mean we must be of it. I mean this not so much in a lofty metaphysical sense as I do as a way of saying that the worlds of matter and the mind, which seem to have us under their dominion and in their control, can be escaped by anyone willing to put forth the necessary effort to leave behind what, under close examination, *makes no sense*.

In this world, there are many people who have decided that the answer to their travails—physical or psycho-logical—is some form of positive thinking or self-affirming religion. Then there are those who, like Freud, believe that since our real problem lies in the unconscious ego, denying the reality of this problem through affirma-tions is not only counterproductive, but dangerous; the solution being to remove our repressions and confront and dismiss the hidden dragons of fear, guilt, and hate. Only

1

thus, they say, can we ever find a personal peace in the midst of the many wars of the world and the mind.

To do this successfully, we need to realize that the real external teacher we are searching for must be recognized as ourselves, then accepted on a daily, or even hourly, basis as a schoolmaster we are no longer too lazy or insipid in outlook to ignore. As a wise leader of ourselves, we should want to adopt the characteristics of the teacher we would have most desired in our formal education: one who was dedicated and firm and who brooked no nonsense, yet was fair, understanding, and patient, and, above all, consistently encouraging and kind.

Through this process, we will eventually encounter our inner Teacher, recognizing the wise outer teacher of ourselves we've become as none other than the reflection of the inner Teacher, realizing we are on a journey, not of the body, but of the mind. This is a journey not of accomplishments, but of undoing; not of learning, but of unlearning all past lessons that had us convinced our mistakes were crimes, that our natural strength had turned inside-out into weakness, and that our purpose on earth was to continually seek to satiate the hungers of a dis-satisfied self in constant need.

Because our potential to learn is beyond measure, it is within our power and nature to overcome our limitations and obstacles to growth, coming at last to remember what we have forgotten: what and "who" we really are.

THE FIRST FLOOR
Or the World of the "I Am"

To begin, let us imagine a metaphorical house with four floors and a cellar representing the physical and psychological worlds of the undeniably self-important "I am." The first floor, where we'll begin this journey, is the temporal world as we know it and as it is, which we will learn are not always the same thing.

This temporal, ground-floor world of "our house" is clearly paranoiac, often, it seems, with just cause. In our world, many countries protect themselves from invasion with armies and navies, which they sometimes use to invade others. Cities and towns safeguard their inhabitants with police officers and sheriff's deputies—people who in turn must be monitored so that they don't slip into abusing the power of the gun. Houses and cars need locks and alarm systems to prevent them from being burglarized or stolen. Women's purses have straps that, in part, are there so they won't be ripped away. Personal information on computers requires elaborate defenses against identity theft. Movies and songs and even ships are being pirated, banks robbed, people kidnapped, children molested, women raped, stores shoplifted, stocks manipulated, pockets picked, and quantities in food and personal care product packages surreptitiously reduced in size without a corresponding reduction in price. Credit card issuers are today's loan sharks. Pharmaceutical companies are often the careless or dullishly unconcerned abusers of the fearful, the miserable, the poor, and the elderly. Our lawmakers usually think first and foremost about being re-elected, a number of them lining their pockets and landing cushy jobs for their relatives and friends, and themselves as well when they leave office. In a general sense, having more—of whatever—than others is seen as good, with competitive, comparative, or judgmental thoughts considered normal, while attacking others is believed to be almost biological in origin. And few seem to look on all this as unnatural and strange.

In the dim-witted world of the first floor, where we grab and seize and blame and keep, we do some commonly accepted, but very strange things. For example, instead of devoting our efforts toward building one comfortable, safe, reliable, fuel-efficient, easily repairable, and relatively inexpensive automobile to get us from place *A* to place *B*—the point of all transportation—we have hundreds of makes and models, because this is what we have seduced ourselves into liking, being also the way car companies make—or sometimes lose—more money. This is no different than supermarkets and megastores being filled to the brim with choices beyond measure in breakfast cereals, personal care products, canned peas, greeting cards, yogurts, and even bottled waters. All this may feed our desires for different experiences, but it is vastly overdone and, due to its complication and duplication, unnecessarily expensive and harmful to the environment.

Don't get me wrong, I'm not against choice, improvement, or reasonable variety. Nor do I want to change the system or robotize tastes. I'm just pointing out how we've allowed the combination of advertising, marketing, and our cravings for better, brighter, and more of what we don't really need to live a good life to confound our good sense and rifle our collective pockets. Another good example of what I find questionable at best for a nation in debt is the billions of dollars the U.S. government spends on space exploration. I'm not opposed to great adventures, the possibility of mining other planets for minerals, or the idea of one day inhabiting Mars. But with countless humans still cold and hungry and sick, and not enough money to help them, the expenditure seems to be at this point "starry-eyed" and pretty unreasonable at best.

These are just a few examples out of many of our uncaring and cannibalistic ways of dealing with one another. We see ourselves with separate interests and, in that, consider ourselves individually as quite important. Having given belief to the absurd idea of differences in intrinsic worth, inequality is no longer seen as absurd because of the power and the attraction of the belief. Once we see ourselves as essentially different, we automatically enter the ugly game of better and worse. Now seemingly separated and, therefore, somewhat desperate, we fight with others in defense of the fatherland of the me, hiding from the realization that in so many varying ways we are acting less charitably than we could and should be. This is the world of "I am very important," a place of constant conflict in which there can never be peace, because everyone is seen as different from everyone else.

In this strange and alien world of separate interests, others often have something that the "I come first" desires, be that something money, intelligence, position, status, a wider circle of friends, influence, power, whatever. And so I am attracted to you, not because I care for you, but because I want some of what you have and I don't. In other words, as a separated "I am" lacking a sense of fullness and completion, I want to rob you, use you, or in some way take from you. In this dog-eat-dog version of reality on the first floor of our metaphorical house, I want what I want when I want it, and if that causes someone else a problem, too bad for him. This includes my using the other as a scapegoat and blaming him for my failures, or even for having what I want and wish for; for if things were really fair, I'd have them and he would not, making him the poverty-stricken supplicant or aspiring thief instead of poor and needy me.

The first floor is the home of hurt and hurting, physically and psychologically, and the refutation of proper perspective found in the idea "I am most important" will never make our bleak and disorienting experience of it other than it is. It is the world of projection of guilt and condemnation of one by the other, a place of continual deception wherein we are convinced we are tormented by harmful actions or words—and not our thinking about them—and are justified in seeking to harm "evil others" in return. It is a place of perversity, degeneracy, stubbornness, and fear, where we, who have been unfaithful to our highest ideals and have lost faith in goodness as absolute, demonstrate in so many ways that we have lost faith in ourselves. And now we, who are at the core—and only the core counts—one and the same, compete and slander and judge and malign, perceiving so many as unworthy because we peer out at the world through the lens of the "I am important," which means those others are not.

Seen without self-deception, this is the reality of the world of the first floor, essentially a cold and cruel place behind its pretensions of otherwise. And the sooner it is seen for the realm of reckless abandonment it is, and yet so cleverly disguises underneath all its "goodness," the sooner its thought system can be exchanged for one where real hope can bloom and not fade away. Only then can we teach and learn the forgotten lesson of everyone's innocence, becoming aware that we, who had lost our way for a while, can follow our true wisdom in a safe passage to what is sensible, feeling deep inside our minds for the remembrance that these words about everyone's innate goodness are not just pretty sentiments, but true. At this point, however, let's not get ahead of ourselves, for we've only begun our exploration, and things have to get worse for a while before they get—unbelievably—better.

THE CELLAR

In the far corner of the first floor, hidden under the deep pile rug of denial, there is a handle to a trapdoor leading down to the cellar. Now, if you think our world of the first floor sounded unattractive at best, it doesn't hold a candle to the wrong-minded and abhorrent thought system of the cellar. Here is where the insanity of working against our own interests is born, bred in the bone, maintained, and kept hidden, with the unavoidable law of compensation— i.e., psychologically speaking, good or bad, you get what you give—completely unseen. Here judgment, the executioner of sameness, sits at the right hand of its progenitor, hate, reigning supreme in the celebration of others' misery our comparative thinking sponsors so eagerly. Deep in the cellar, it is always Halloween without the treats, the palace of threat wherein shadows of fear weave their dark magic spells, the homeland and source of our nightmares and daymares alike.

At this Halloween party, everyone who wants to play the game of vanity is presented with a costume, a mask, and an opportunity to pretend to be other than he or she is. In the prideful bacchanalia of the cellar, those rejoicing at others' misfortunes have become ruinously rooted, so identified with their costumes they believe that without them they would be nothing, perceiving punishment or extinction as their certain future in payment for all their wicked ways. In this fantasy world, not only accusation and blame, but endowing others with confidences they are likely to betray, is customary—the disguised and nefarious purpose of the endowment being the wish for the betrayal, the subsequent agonizing over it hiding its relishable intent. Here we find the sickly source of the standards by which we judge other celebrants' sincerity, holding them in contempt without due process, because that is both the culture and common manner of the costumed people of "Halloween."

"A devilish lair" is the proper nomenclature for the deviously wrought cellar, its terrible influence coming from the mind's involvement in a tissue of lies, a cobweb deftly spun and held together by the beguiling legions of fraud. And it is here that we, now thoroughly confused by our identifications with our costumes, have descended into anarchy, "loving" selectively and hating frequently, caught in a mindset that is half falsity, with the other half deception, no longer aware of what we do, with only the faintest glimmerings of hope to be perceived in the darkness. Please do not think that these words are merely hyperbolic, for until we become willing to look at the wrong-minded bacchanalia for what it is, we will remain its unknowing captives, with even our best efforts to think positively merely covering it over, serving equally, then, the purpose of keeping us away from the return to sense.

In the cellar, wrong-mindedness is firmly in charge and rules with an iron fist. Here, victims, giving great credence to their self-pitying thoughts, attempt to victimize their victimizers with an accusatory woundedness, each in their self-given martyrdom doing their best to return the pain they are certain they have received. There is no mercy to be found in the dark thought system of the cellar, only using and accusing and abusing, with everyone experiencing deprivation because the beneficence of giving has been turned on its head. The cellar is a state of mind so bereft of decency that all who live in accordance with its lessons end up feeling as unwelcome as would orphans of the cold. In this place of corrupted thinking, unkindness is seen as merely self-protective, the fearful hating all those who are either like or unlike them, the gods they worship necessarily perceived as cruel as themselves.

Who but the delusional would persist in seeking satisfaction in a bacchanalia of *schadenfreude*, their enjoyment fueled by finding pleasure in another's seeming unworthiness or greater woes? Who but the unbalanced could think that being the prudent third little pig, looking down his nose at the less-industrious or foolish first and second little pigs, could leave him with anything other than the unpleasant conviction that he, too, is a pig? There *is* no hope of finding peace or pleasure in a state of mind that has banished the reality of our underlying sameness, having traded it in for the idea of a personal specialness and all the horrors of selfishness that come in its wake.

In the cellar, it is not understood that taking seriously the belief there is a separated self to have a problem with others is everyone's real problem. We want the world to stop pestering us, unaware that the great lesson of the world is to learn we are pestering ourselves, slowly becoming aware that nothing outside our wrong-mindedness, which is essentially a choice, has any "pestering power" at all. The introductory phase of the process of escape from our conditioning that believes otherwise begins not by our changing anything, but by looking with honesty at how deeply engaged we are in the story of the puny fraud we now think of as "me," and how enamored we are of the idea of specialness and the story of self. After a while, understanding better our love affair with our invented self-importance, it becomes evident why the messages of those who have left the cellar behind so often fall on deaf ears. We're not really interested in learning that we are the problem to be solved. We want to find the evidence that "proves" someone else is the problem. And this because, despite all our busyness, we don't really want the problem solved.

Looked on with level-headedness, this is lunacy. But not to the already unbalanced. To us, there is no gulf between our way of thinking and reason to be crossed. To those of us who plod along in a daily depression mixed with fits of excitement, conquering others is a routine we have become so accustomed to, we now experience it as, and call it, "life." And rash and presumptuous indeed appears to be anyone who has the temerity to question what the self-convinced insist everyone accept as so.

Because fear is the emotion of the cellar, all who are caught up in the belief in its values find themselves unavoidably uncertain and anxious. It is very difficult for those caught up in a thought system that makes the trivial seem significant to entertain the idea that their self-importance is merely an expression of the thinking of their own unbalanced minds. Or to accept that every foggy illusion of self is, no matter its achievements, actually accomplishing nothing at all. It takes a while to adjust to the idea that life as we are living it is devoid of meaning for the simple reason that it makes no sense. Yet it is exactly the recognition and the acceptance of this lack of meaning that is the hope, and the only hope, of all who lost touch with reason and its good sense the moment they agreed to join in partnership with the carelessness so prevalent in the revelry of the cellar's bacchanalia.

What is not understood by minds absorbed in what poses as "thinking" in this state of wrong-mindedness are the consequences of conflicting with others who are, under their costumes, in reality like us and all the same. Once value has been given to striving after glory for glory's sake, we are automatically in the condition of believing ourselves to be in opposition to the interests of all who are thinking in like ways. It is this belief in a personal importance, taken as deserved, that is the primordial and perennial bane of our existence, the hardest obstacle to be overcome by all who see the loss of specialness as if it were death instead of the doorway to life.

And so, what clarity of mind begins to show us is that accepting the thinking of the cellar and letting it direct our behavior in the seeming world of one or the other— symbolized, as we've seen, by the first floor—is to doom ourselves to an existence lived out in the shadows of fear's excitement and its always ensuing despair. Is this monotonous irregularity a fit inheritance for us? Are we really meant to live a life of constant competition, comparison, and a disguised love of self, watching in dismay as all our satisfactions begin to flee the very moment they arrive? Surely such an impasse cannot have permanent reality; there must be an escape from the cellar, the shadowy first floor, and the terrible trap of the avaricious "I am."

THE SECOND FLOOR, PART I

The second floor symbolizes the place and time, where and when, we begin to realize we've been, to put it mildly, misguided, now going "above" our enslavement to the material world of the first floor to start living a life of the mind. If the first floor is, in effect, unknowing Sisyphean labor, the second is the dawning realization that the boulder of narcissistic self-love can be pushed over the hill in Hades, to roll down and far away on the other side. Self-importance is the problem to be overcome, all its memories of "good" and "evil," granted and received, like "Tales from the Crypt." Look at the world it generates and we unthinkingly venerate: a place filled with rocks to be thrown, clubs to be wielded, knives to be thrust, guns to be shot, and bombs to be exploded. The first floor is not a world but a madhouse. And we who continue to participate in this form of insanity can be said to be making one thing alone, and that is progress to nowhere.

In this common dilemma, everyone's real need is to meet someone who no longer takes for granted the primitive illusion we wander in, a peaceful someone who will remind us that to attempt to hurt others for their transgressions is to join them in pain. It is only when we gain an understanding of the difficulty of our struggle with having made specialness our god and pride our present love that we are on our way to regaining our sense. Our real journey is out of the coma of disguised self-hatred, not into one of greater depression in the ever-disappointing world of the first floor. Only those who are confused attack fellow travelers, or fall for the equally brutal seduction of condemning those who do. It is only when all are seen as trying as hard as is presently possible, even when those efforts may seem pitiful, that we can perceive them beyond their beliefs and their behaviors as still worthy, which is the only fair definition of what they—and we—are.

To put the concept of progressing up from the first floor in a different context, let's imagine that, once again metaphorically speaking, we are all engaged in a cleverly designed and nightmarish game being played in a shrouded and icy cold river, a game that may seem, at times, to be stimulating, but one that never brings comfort to our minds or joy to our hearts. The game we play is basically one of plunging others under the surface—in effect, "putting them down"—in order to demonstrate the reality of our self-determined superiority. And, when not this, one of hanging onto those we perceive as stronger in order to stay afloat, accomplishing little more than affirming our belief in our own supposed inferiority. The game of manipulation and using is formulated to give us moments of vanishing pleasure, which, while distracting us from our shivering, is actually quite unsettling. For no matter how vigorous and consuming or even "successful" are our efforts, the icy river the game is played in never warms up in the slightest degree. Once this is seen, the logical question becomes, is there someplace more suited to what we want, meaning warmer?

If we are truly fed up with our lives in this cold-hearted place of vain pursuits and sincere in our questioning, we can look beyond what we've been accepting as the only reality and perceive that on the far side of the fog bank of our confusion, there is a distant shore. To our tired eyes, this shore seems far, far away, and there are cliffs to be climbed should we manage to get there, but above these cliffs, we can see there is light and warmth and dry air. And while it doesn't appear there are any separated selves on that distant shore, the prospective exchange of a benumbed personal self for an impersonal concept, such as one of light, seems more promising than remaining as not much more than a disappearing ice cube in the isolating, cold game of how important, by comparison, we can grow to be.

Yet there is still value to be found in the icy river's hard-hearted game. And that value stems from letting its constant failures to satisfy teach us to not want its pseudo-rewards any longer. To turn the tables on the designer of the game—ultimately ourselves—is to use the game for a new purpose, that being to free ourselves from the terrible trap we willingly walked into. This is the only aim that deserves our devotion, all the other "gifts" of the game being mockeries of what we truly deserve and can come to realize we really want. Escape from the trap is the goal of all who have grown wise enough to see the game's secreted cleverness for what it is and who are no longer captivated by the idea of discovering lasting contentment in a place where it was never born and, therefore, can never be.

To find ourselves again on that distant shore as we truly are is so important that everything else pales into insignificance. With this possibility in sight, all our mistakes can be properly regarded as no more than learning experiences, and all our successes as the same, in reality no greater in value than the winter's snow that came only to melt away in the spring. It takes time to learn, and willingness to accept, that the hidden name for money, power, fame, or pleasure is "more," and nothing else. Yet it is precisely our overindulgence in any of these idols of the marketplace that demonstrates overindulgence never works and cannot bring happiness—balance becoming much more attractive as extremes are experienced as eventually tormenting the extremist.

In a more balanced way of living, where selfishness no longer rules the day, the other person becomes more important than the transaction, no matter how important the transaction may seem. This does not mean we never say no—sensible people often do just that. Rather, it means we are growing in awareness of the fact that if we seek to deprive others, we inevitably will interpret our losses not as no big deal, but as retribution for our prior selfishness. We should not underestimate the significance or the depth of this problem, or the all-inclusiveness of its only real solution. Only faith in the underlying worth of all will undermine our fear of freedom from the self, returning to the forefront of our aspiration the balance that accompanies fairness and respect.

In the clarity of mind fostered by this gentler way of living, we begin to understand our real upset with others as coming from pointing an accusing finger and not from what they've done or said. The fact is that when we become disturbed because of another's expression of selfishness, an expression of his or her own inner disturbance, we've unknowingly married ourselves to it. The solution is to admit to ourselves as quickly as possible that we have done this and then divorce it without divorcing the person in our minds. A helpful way to think of this is that another's mistake, reacted to emotionally, must also be our mistake, our reaction being the proof we have secretly apprenticed ourselves to the weak-minded desire to feel unjustly treated. This desire to play the victim is another expression of the confusion that has made us believe that we are the subjects and not the authors of the unlikeable stories we find ourselves engrossed in.

Only the part of our minds that feels inadequate comes up with complaints about others, as only learning to stand free of our need that things be different provides a refuge from such a state of imbalance. When we learn to see in a different way, it will become clearer that our feelings are inner directed and so can be redirected, that they are never the masters of a balanced mind. At this point we can more honestly admit that we have been using the mistakes of others as convenient distractions from our own undealt-with problems, recognizing that this shady activity has done nothing to relieve our pain or reduce our shame.

Taking what seems like advantage of others' errors in this way is counterproductive to our own mental health. When someone becomes fearful and acts in an aggressive manner, and the self-imposed hypnosis, or wrong-mindedness, we labor under fiercely commands, "This is unjust! Get him back! Give it to him! Give him hell!," and in a

Pavlovian way, we come stumbling out of our neutral corner to engage in the fight, we are wrong. This is the cycle we must learn to break out of. This is the urge of the ego we must learn to resist. This, and not the other person, is what needs healing through bringing our minds back to their senses where, by shunning harmfulness, we can again become helpful to everyone, including ourselves.

To permanently escape from the terrible swamp of selfishness, we must accept that every equal—and *everyone* is our equal—deserves favorable consideration regardless of his or her behavior, the behavior simply witnessing to a present state of mind. Disturbed behavior points back to a disturbed mind, and the only helpful response to a disturbed mind is one that refuses the invitation to join in the foolishness and add fuel to a fire that should be robbed of support, not fed by more madness.

To be of real assistance calls for a willingness to respect another's right to be wrong for as long as the fear of being otherwise remains dominant in his mind. This means that when someone becomes dogmatic and gets upset and insists on remaining so, we must learn to look beyond his stubbornness to the fear of being without his current dogma that is its ultimate source. So the other makes a wrong turn in his mind and thereby becomes frightened and, consequently, hostile, perhaps even blaming us for his misstep. In *all* such situations, the reasonable part of our minds says, "And what does this other person's mistake possibly have to do with me?" Yet, the question here is not whether our good sense is saying this, but rather are we willing to listen.

If we do listen, and then begin to throw out our first-floor furniture of judgment, regret, blame, and concern, it will seem at times as if there is nothing left to return or hold on to. Yet, the transition from the belief system of the defensive self, whose "buttons" can be pushed by anyone and anything, to the understanding there is but one button that can be pushed, and that one by no one but ourselves, is unfamiliar only at first. We are accustomed to the idea of being wounded, but that is only because we have *wanted* to feel wounded, being wounded "perfect proof" there is a self-important and separated "me" to be wounded. In other words, if we are wounded emotionally, we are doing it to ourselves.

All this is akin to the idea that when another attacks us in any way, attendant to that attack, there appears—in our imaginations—to be a psychological arrow aimed directly at our hearts. And yet, because we *alone* choose how we feel, when another launches their psychological arrow at us, no matter what it may seem like, that arrow always falls short. We each, however, have a hidden sheath of arrows in our back pockets, and when the other's arrow is in the air flying toward us, and yet landing before it reaches us, we, with a rapidity so practiced and swift we no longer see it, reach into the sheath, grab an arrow, plunge it into our chests, and then pronounce to ourselves, to others, and to the attacker, "Look what has been done to a poor dear like me." This is the real secret of our emotional woundedness, and if we are unwilling to acknowledge it, we are not really justified in our anger and complaints.

When we arrive at the condition of no longer allowing the insulting behaviors of the disturbed to influence us, we will realize it was exactly their mistakes that helped us to get in touch with our blamefulness and to reach beyond all thoughts of reproach. Once we conclude that we are truly unaffected by the words and actions of others unless we give them the power to move us, we will see in a new light and exchange the past curses of our "enemies" for present gratitude to those we can now recognize as friends. This is what life in the game is really about, our becoming honest enough to admit that when we are feeling insulted by a person or put upon by fate, it is because we *want* to feel that way, and that there is *no other* generator of our experience. Accepting this is what it means to become responsible. And what else would we, who want to become grownups, do?

To wipe clean the pages of the mental diaries in which we have recorded everyone's mistakes is to free ourselves from the imbalance wrought by the defenses of self-hatred and to begin to regain our equilibrium. Here we learn that the root of shame is blame, as the root of blame is shame. This is the way to peace we must follow, our highest aspiration leading us through the clouds of seeming guilt to the brightly lit mountaintop of innocence, where all still-darkened valleys of memory and misthought are perceived for the self-deceptions they are. From here, the temptations of the wrong mind to justify anger and grief have lost their grim appeal, no longer seen as offering anything worth abandoning our place on high. And when we forget, and it seems they have us in their talons, it is soon recognized this is only because we have again fallen for the deception that says the episodic excitement of the contest in the icy river is metal more attractive than the contentment that comes with forgiveness without blame.

To find ourselves without the necessary confidence to resist the pull of condemnation of equals—self-condemnation in disguise—is a direct result of identifying ourselves with the sickly notion "I am more valuable than you." Vanity is insanity, everyone who believes in it as justified, an unknowing prisoner of self-worship. Yet the journey out of this queerly designed, misanthropic, and conceited thought system of a personal importance is as short and as swift as is our sincerity in facing up to our dishonesty. We're one and all charlatans, professors of the belief in a concept of self that has no cause for faith, self-inventions imagined by what itself is an invention. And here we find ourselves in an ugly game that has never made us content, because what gets its meaning from outdoing others is discontented in nature from inception to end.

Seeing everyone as alike in our common need to escape the enthrallment of the game of "me first" will lead to the awareness that all of us are in the same mighty struggle to escape the deep enchantment of the supposed rewards of the selfish "I am." It is the hidden desire to be special that keeps us caught in the throes of competition and comparison, as it is the acceptance of our underlying sameness that will show us we are imprisoned by nothing more than our own wish for the impossible, and, thus, as free or as bound as we will to be. Therefore, since freedom is the only real need of anyone in a trap, it is freedom, specifically from condemnation, we should offer to each and all. One practical way of describing this idea from the standpoint of our daily living is as follows:

Imagine that there are three "doorways" in our minds, any of the three awaiting our choice.

- The doorway on the left calls to us to enter and dwell in the over, gone, and no-longer-here past, the place of memory and grief wherein our shame and pain moan and groan in their ever-wearying lament of "you, he, she, they, or I, should—or should not—have done or said that," the underlying implication being there is a guilty someone who needs to repent and face punishment.

- The doorway on the right also invites us to come in, leading all who enter into an imaginary and future world of worry and want, where fear, like a broken record, insistently rasps, "I hope I get this and I hope I don't get that, and above all, if someone is to be punished, I hope it won't be me, even though deep in the background something keeps whispering it will."

- The third doorway is the one directly in front of us, offering welcome into the quietness of living fully in the distinct world of the present hour. Here we are truly welcome for the rest of our days, with the only rule for inclusion in its safety being *be kind to all who enter, be that in thought or in form.*

In the present hour, everything that shows up—in memory, thought, or form—can be conceived of as an envelope with a message inside; in each case the sender and the receiver of the meaning the message seems to provide being no one other than ourselves. This is first understood intellectually, and then recognized as needing to be practiced by learning what it means to stand back from, which doesn't mean to deny, but rather to watch, our reactions to everything that happens. Only watching our minds will lead us out of responding to misthought like automatons, returning us to the remembrance of ourselves as decision-making minds. In present living, our pseudo-connection with the self made of pride and shame begins to dissolve, with faith in our ability to escape its clutches—really our own false desires—slowly replacing everything else. It is this capacity to choose the freedom to live in the present hour we want to learn to respect, not the meaningless pulls of a misconstrued past or an imaginary future that suggest it is really possible to live in what is not here. It is in our willingness to accept things as they are that we at last get what we want, because we want what we get, using everything that happens as means to awaken to our unappreciated power to learn.

As we practice observing our reactions in the present hour, we begin to realize what actually happens with everyone we meet is that *we choose* to look at him rightly or we choose to look at him wrongly, our decision as to how to think about him *predating and predicating our perception.* This means that our relationship with him is not what we think: being not really with him, but with our minds' decision about him. Therefore, what is doubt about him other than a witness to our lack of faith in ourselves? In other words, unless we had first chosen to see ourselves as unworthy, we could never have seen the other as unworthy, our perception being a mirror of that inner decision and not a fact at all.

Those who choose rightly, and have seen others as friends, are no longer competitive. They race to race when to race is what's called for, but they don't race to beat others even when they win. They live in the understanding that victory and loss have no relationship to their happiness, more interested in seeing rightly than in how they are seen, becoming aware that under the multifarious disguises of the "I am," we remain as we were, which is simply the same. People with truly peaceful minds have come to the conclusion that winning cared about is actually losing, and that losing—and winning—uncared about is the real sign of advancement. There is no victory possible in the icy river's game of self-interest. No matter the size or number of the trophies acquired by those who value accumulation, the grand-prize winner is still as cold to the bone as the one with the smallest gain.

The true gift of worldly success, material gain, or the approbation of others comes with the discovery there is literally no hope of satisfaction there. The great, and *great* it is, reward for working hard to improve ourselves arrives on the day we realize that there is only a self-invented "I am important" to be rewarded at all. This unexpected insight is quite shocking at first, because it goes counter to everything we've been led to believe matters, not only by others, but by the story of the riches to be found in "self-improvement" we've bought into heretofore.

The big surprise waiting to greet us is not just that we are not what we had thought, but that, since *all* our dualistic functioning has been in our imaginations, we haven't done anything—good or bad—at all. But don't read this hastily, as if it portends oblivion. Rather think of it as the doorway to the remembrance of faith in our reality as minds, or lights. Our journey through the world of time is not what it appears, one of bettering our condition within it, but rather one of exiting the hypnosis that has kept us locked up in the belief we are not the authors of our stories, but the characters in them. From the freedom of this more-elevated vantage point, we will continue playing our chosen roles, but without taking so seriously the many dark tales of the "me."

Now we live as we've lived before, but more quietly, at this point dedicated first and foremost to the maintenance of our peace of mind. Here our histories, filled to the brim with achievement and failure, having fulfilled their purpose of helping us return to the present where alone we are, no longer need to be dwelled upon, evaluated, or even thought of as important. In the true here and now, found only without the restrictions imposed by the time-bound "me," it is understood that the admiration or the insults of others have only the significance that we provide them. And so whether they place the laurel wreath upon our heads or ask us to return our medals, it is really all the same.

The good news about this is not just that our supposed heroics of mind and seeming defeats are self-fabricated, but that *all* the evil thoughts we remember from the past are but *stories* we put there and can as easily remove. To accept this, it is not necessary for us to say, "I am meaningless," but only to see that the concept of self we are fixated on is no more than a story we have made up and are continuing to pretend to be.

Stories are contrivances meant to keep us engrossed in drama, so we won't wake up to what we are doing to ourselves. Here in a world we might as well call Storyland, each of us is living in a fiction of our own making, perceiving what we think, seeing as we choose, yet convinced there really is a separated world of meaning "out there." Recognizing that what we had thought of as objective perceptions were no more than subjective observations comes as somewhat of a revelation. Up to this point, we were certain we were dealing with reality. With this new insight, it starts to dawn on us that if we are actually providing the content to what we see, quite possibly all we perceive is merely an illusion, with no more reality than has a mirage in a desert. Yet, once we realize this would also mean that *all* our remembrances of pain and shame are equally no more than chapters in a fable, freedom from a trap so convincing it seemed forever inescapable can be heard to knock with authority on a door within we had forgotten existed.

That we have been stupefied by our own deviousness does not mean our stupefaction is a permanent condition, because in reality, like all other stories, the story of the storyteller behind this charade has no power we have not granted it. Once we give up this unseen validation of the storyteller by ceasing to believe that any of its mindless stories of duality could possibly be true, the fact that we—as deluded minds—are the sole supporters of these hateful tales is finally exposed. Recognizing this is a steppingstone toward returning our attention to the minds that are supporting the production of this entire fantasy: story problems, story selves, storytellers, and all else we encounter in this scheme of delusion we are so "happily" engaged in. At this point, we'll be able to do something meaningful about this dilemma of wanting what ends up doing little more than capturing our attention, relinquishing our fears of letting go of what is not and never was.

The reality of what has happened in the delusional tale of the separated self is that nothing real has happened, because *it's all made up*. All of our fitful meanderings in the fetid fields of self-centeredness have led nowhere. Our greatest successes have been colossal self-deceptions for the simple reason that they have failed to pacify our restless minds. Our exulted-in "victories," where the insanity of our vanity has always been the grand marshal of the parade, have brought nothing but guilt and its sorrow in their wake. Our frantic participation in the game of one or the other in the icy river has resulted in little more than turning our hearts as cold as riverbed stones. And all our striving for gain and glory has accomplished nothing more than to turn us away from our true goal: the remembrance of what we truly are. This amnesia is our real problem, and we have no other.

Now, obviously, before we can solve a problem, we must first recognize that we have a problem, which our second-floor perspective can help us to do. And if our problem is that we are lost in a story of self without intrinsic meaning, then part of the process of remembering what we've forgotten would be to accept what we've done and are, right now, continuing to do to ourselves. Could we, perhaps, be not awake, but dreaming? Consider carefully the world of mayhem that surrounds us. Next, look at how easily disturbed we can become when something or someone violates our picture of how things should be. How could such instability be other than the result of confusion? And what can confusion given meaning be but a tale told by an idiot? In other words, part of a senseless story or dream.

That the world is apparent and tangible in what we think of as our waking state does not prove that it is real other than to the thought system in the mind dependent on evidence from the senses. The ice cream cones we ate when we were six were apparent and tangible then, too, but where are they now? And if we cannot place them now, can we be sure they were ever real and not just apparitions in a self-fabricated dream? Or can we be certain, because we have pictures and letters and memories, that they are anything other than more pieces in the ongoing saga of the self? Can temporal things that do not last, e.g., ice cream cones, incidents, bodies, be more than ephemeral appearances? Is our difficulty with entertaining these thoughts that question what we are so sure of, that, if we did so, it would open to question the reality of ourselves as we are "mostly" certain we are?

If the authenticity of the self we've embraced is unsubstantiated, other than by sense evidence, thought, and memory, and advancing the interests of this so-called "me" has not led to peace of mind, might we not be better off if we have been mistaken about what we are and where our happiness is to be found? What if *real* happiness lies *only* in the exchange of the coldness of selfishness for the warmth of shared interests? Surely by now we've realized that since excitement over beating others always brings deflation, disappointment, and greater yearning in its wake, it cannot be anything other than disguised suffering in the making. The adage "what goes up must come down" explains why those who strive for victory in the war of specialness end up frustrated and are so often discontent and bereft.

Ultimately, the central problem for all of us is having chosen to identify with our images, once in the morass, no longer realizing these are just tales of misadventures being told by the senseless storyteller of "how important I am." With even the glimmering of an understanding that it is in our minds' engagement with the illusory that our problems begin and must end, we can start to use unpleasant situations for their hitherto unseen purpose: to show us dentified we are with this idol of personhood we keep defending and, obviously, still secretly adore. In this new interpretation of what relationships are for, and how value can be found in every circumstance, the enemy once perceived to be the cause of our distress can now be thought of as a helper, which is what, to all desirous of awakening from their wrathful sleep of separate interests, he or she is.

"Return to your natural wisdom," our good sense quietly says. "Raise your head above the mind-benumbing water in the icy river's game of pride and turn toward the shore of modesty, where alone our sameness can be found. Your purpose is to remember your true reality, not to become more adept at proving you are not what you are and are what you are not. Find the freedom that comes with putting others first. Give up the idea of conflict as worthwhile, and refuse to pay attention to anyone who tells you it is important to become number one in any of Storyland's many races to nowhere. Come home. You don't belong out there in that cold and icy river, trying to drown your brother's story because he, who had no respect for his own story of self, couldn't offer respect to yours. Start now on your return and, when you become doubtful of your worth and seem to lose your way, refuse to remain in any such quagmire. Instead, pick yourself up, and firmly say to yourself 'Next!' and then begin again. Leave chaos and its turmoil behind starting now, and when you forget your purpose and slip back into mindlessness, calmly leave again, over and over, until remembering to smile at your lapses is all that remains as a response to your forgetting, and self-recrimination can no longer claw and bite."

THE SECOND FLOOR, PART II

The terrible game of self-advancement is replete with people striving to be special, absent the understanding that to be special is to be separated, to be separated is to be apart, to be apart is to be isolated, to be isolated is to be alone, to be alone is to end up frightened, and really nothing more. These are the ones in need of welcome to everyone's home away from home in the sanctuary of the cathedral of light of the present hour, the very ones who, in our faith in good reason for their inclusion, will show us that we, too, belong here in this quiet place of comfort, where condemnation of equals no longer has meaning or appeal.

As we've seen, every encounter with another, be it in person or in our minds, is as *we* would have it be. Therefore, what is important in Storyland is not what happens, but how we choose to perceive and respond to it. Clearly, the reality of everyone entranced by the guile of the game is that we all have been mean-minded at times. Recognizing this as a form of blindness, or ignorance, seeing it in others gives us the opportunity to forgive ourselves for our own past—or present—mistakes of a similar kind. In this way of perceiving, when another makes a mistake, it becomes an opportunity for us to give what—in our own forms of distress—we would most like to receive. Here other people's impatience, arrogance, or hostility is seen differently, this time as a plea for understanding, allowing us to offer them what they are really asking for and need. Not because we are in possession of something they have not, but because we are aware that the gentleness of mercy belongs to everyone or it belongs to no one and, therefore, is their right and due. Thus we can help without the bitter "aid" of conde-scension from an implied better, or "hero," and so be of real benefit to all.

We want to learn what it means to do the right thing, not the heroic thing, for many times they are not the same. The "heroic" thing often is done first for ourselves, i.e., for improving our images in the eyes of others, or ourselves, even when it—coincidentally or purposely—benefits others. The right thing is done for the betterment of all. It may be, and in some cases will be, less popular. But it won't be selfish, because it won't be about improving our images or about being liked. And so it will be truly helpful—even to those who don't believe so and complain. In other words, it won't be personal, and so it can be sensible, and to be sensible, again, is a natural step on our journey to reason and the wisdom within from which it comes.

What better way to learn that we are truly generous—and not just conditionally so—than to see each opportu-nity to be helpful to the temporarily bereft for the chance it is to be of real help to ourselves? Being generous and helpful and kind are gifts from the natural order to the natural order and, therefore, gifts to everyone involved. As giving of our time to those who ask for it makes time worthwhile, so laying aside selfishness as unwanted eliminates the seeming power of neediness to keep us in the belief we are bereft. These are the ways for us to learn that a generosity that is not all-inclusive is a limitation, another fulsome trick of the wrong-minded thinking that emanates from the unexposed cellar of the mind.

As we are progressing along the path of learning to master ourselves, there will be more times than we would like when we get perturbed by the doings of others and find ourselves wanting to lash out at them. When this happens, and it will, the reasonable question to ask ourselves is whether we want the guilt that acting on this—deceptively—righteous impulse is sure to bring. And even if at that moment we give in to temptation and allow ourselves to act on our "justified" rage, we'll at least be able to trace back the reason why we feel so lousy later. This dedication to honesty will eventually save us, because it will help us to both restrain and retrain ourselves by recognizing that our murderousness toward others is, in fact, first and foremost directed at ourselves. This, in turn, will lead to the realization that the mature and truly contented are merely those previously discontented children who saw the game of kill or be killed for what it is and refused to play with fire any longer.

We may believe that in order to be content we just need to remain where we are in the game and do better: live here or there, drive this or that, be pitied for our sufferings, appreciated for all the good we do, or find him or her or the treasure we seek. But unless we are mere stories of self, *none* of this is true. As discussed earlier, what we are truly in search of cannot be found in any form of acquisition, be it of goods, approvals, or external confirmations of worth. Nor can the misery of our feelings that we are like "fish out of water" be lessened by reaching a higher level of status in the game of "pay attention to me." The real answer to our seeming dilemma—that happiness and peace of mind are one and the same—is not elusive. It's just that we, who still value excitement over quietness, don't want to hear it. And so, instead of directing our efforts toward getting out of the cage of selfishness, we keep trying to make being in it more palatable.

The "reality principle" for the reasonable is to learn to live without complaint with what is. In this sense, if we truly wanted peace of mind, we would have it. And since we don't yet have it, at least not consistently, either it doesn't exist consistently, or it does and we still have work to do to return to where it lives. To most players of the fierce game of self-importance in the icy river, finding the way to higher highs and not-so-lower lows seems to be the most sensible pursuit possible. Maintaining a state of balance between what the game defines as reason for rejoicing or dismay seems so foreign to their thought systems, their first response is usually, "Oh, that would be so boring." Yet what could be more boring than the constant mood swings between excitement and despair that accompany winning and losing trophies made of vapors of ice so evanescent they are already disappearing as they are raised aloft?

Something not usually considered is that, logically speaking, the only way for one to have a sensible investment in outcomes would be to know what outcome would be best. Yet, examined honestly, based on irrefutable evidence, often we do not know. Therefore, investment in outcomes is actually mental sophistry somewhat cleverly posing as sense. To become overly exercised when we don't get our way is akin to a child having a tantrum over not receiving what might well have been deleterious to his or her health or well-being. Yet, for as long as we are hooked into identifying with our stories of self and caught in the notion of being a person of importance, the condition is inevitable. And what is the way out of all this? Not to deny that we have egos, but to deny our egos the right to have us.

The corollary of the thought there are things that can make us feel better than we naturally should is the thought there are things that can make us feel worse than we should. The rejection of these thoughts divorces pleasure and pain from significance, marrying us to the idea there is no difficulty or excitement that cannot be rendered impotent in its power to disturb by disbelief in the ego's commentary behind its form. The truth is that what goes on in Storyland has nothing to do with what we really are. However, being afraid—really unwilling, all fear being resistance—to accept that everything that goes on here is neutral, we keep placing meaning on what, until we engage with it, has none.

Our mission is to come to a complete disbelief in the reality of anything other than Perfection, to return to the remembrance of absolute goodness alone as supreme. All else is no more than scary stories being told around the campfires of hell. And this we learn through the process of discerning how the best among us look on and treat the—

seeming—worst among us, anything less than that level of generosity speaking to the "truth" of differences, which can be spoken of only in lies. With this as our aim, all other lesser goals, or achievements in the game, are found to be useful only in demonstrating their inability to satisfy completely and, therefore, their inability to satisfy at all. This is how we uncover the connection between investment and disappointment, learning to shun the first because of the bitter taste of the latter.

As we begin to regroup and allow our innate honesty its deserved status as a dear friend, it will gently show us how confused we actually are and why. At this point, we can cease trying to make sense out of the always puzzling, realizing that since it all fades away, it must be untrue, and if it's untrue, it's untrue, and cannot, in reality, be anything else. Clearly, *everything* in Storyland decays and, sooner or later, is lost from sight forever. How, then, can *any* of it have intrinsic meaning? If we think about it, everyone and everything here—be it animate or inanimate—is like a balloon with the air—slowly or rapidly—leaking out, with, in the end, the balloon itself disintegrating and disappearing as well. And yet, this parade of passing balloons— the forms and the events and the circumstances of Storyland—has neatly served the purpose of capturing our attention so completely we never question that which seems worthy of our interest and devotion only while we are still trying to make sense out of what is little more than moonshine.

Waking up to what has been a servile acquiescence to the demands of our self-centeredness is to perceive that we've been wandering around in a state of delirium. In our self-induced narcosis, we now have amnesia about the fact that the *only* legitimate description of each thing that comes to sight or mind in the passing parade is that it is not. What disappears could not really have been there to begin with, the only definition possible for its opposite, the ineffable Truth, being that which is changeless and lasts forever. "Truth is" means that all else must be untrue, making our deep concerns about the "everything else" no more than defenses constructed to protect the reality of a "fallen self" that does not exist. For there to have been a "fall," there must have been an edge to have fallen from or a bottom to have fallen through. Yet, if Truth is, and is all there is, then in truth, there is nothing else, and so there cannot really have been a fall. Nor, with that, can there be any such thing as a consequence for believing in a completely unreal fallen self. And so the story of "me" must be no more than the product of an unbelief in the Possible in which the impossible has supposedly taken place, undone by emerging from the cocoon of confusion in which such seeming isolation seems either desirable or possible.

It is through the willing surrender of belief in what we made that we erase what interferes with the awareness of what we are. Undoing our dubious connection with the histrionic and dissembling story of self won't lead to loss of identity. How can there be loss in refusing belief to something that outside our imaginations doesn't exist? Or anything but gain in peace of mind as we begin to recognize ourselves, beyond the deception of form, as being no different than others, all of us lights, or minds, doing our best to remember we are the same in truth and therefore really One? Our rebuttal of the constant call for acceptance of such inclusion is like our refusing to accept the honor of first place in the ultimate beauty contest because we would have to share it with everyone else. Can such a defense of the hope for specialness ever be made reasonable in any way at all?

Surrounded by the vast fog of ignorance generated by our sickly desires to count for more than others, we have been wandering about in the first-floor shadows of the odd notion that betrayal of wholeness and separation into specialness are not only possible, but have actually been accomplished. Yet, how could we have betrayed an all-encompassing and undifferentiated unity that we, if we are real at all, must have been one with and still are? In other words, the rejection of something without opposite is quite impossible; that is, other than in fictional stories being told by a fictional storyteller. Nothing has happened to our changeless reality, because nothing *can* happen to the changeless Truth. And what is this vanishing image we have been identifying with? No more than a false claim that nothing can become something through a comatose repetition of demand in an inconceivable storm of thought, what is and all there is leaving no room for an authentic conception of what is not and can never be.

In a practical sense, accepting this usually translates into our continuing to do whatever we had been doing in the Land of Nod, only now more efficiently and peacefully than before because we are less encumbered by our old hang-ups and thwarted desires. And this, while becoming more and more aware that what we seem to see and react to in Storyland is invented by us. This increasing sense of responsibility leads to a far greater sensitivity to the rights of others, from the boss at work to the bagboy in the supermarket, and on to every family member, relative, or any others we engage with, no matter how trouble troublesome at the moment they may be. At this point, we begin to understand that our judgments, negative emotions, and defensiveness are like snakes in the grass hoping to capture our awareness and drag it away from the respect for our equals that will return us to respect for ourselves. Here, too, as in the earlier "arrow" example, we come closer to the conclusion that giving in to feelings of being wounded, betrayed, or put upon come not from others' actions or inaction, but from our own hidden desire to be treated shabbily—that he may be the bad guy and not us.

Our real best interests lie not in finding "reasons" for our selfishness, but in learning to look beyond the obfuscation of form to the commonality of the light, or right mind, we share. From here, we can offer everyone both inclusion and welcome, along with respect for the difficulties we all encounter in waking up out of our dreams of separation and the nightmarish idea of "I am more important than you." Now we can demonstrate that leaving the cruel game in the icy river and swimming toward the warm shore are possible. Yet to succeed at this most important of tasks, we must keep in the forefront of our minds the thought that when another "bites" in any way, it is because he or she has become fearful, and then to practice responding to the fear and not the bite.

Deep within the minds of those who attack and hate and even murder, there is a plea that is saying, "I would *never* speak or act this way if I had not lost my good sense. And since it is clear that I have, would you please, please be the one who, by remaining sensible enough not to take what I'm doing personally, shows me that right-mindedness still exists and can be chosen for, even by someone like me?" And deep within our own minds, and beyond all our defenses against remaining reasonable in the face of attack, there is something in us that knows fulfilling this request alone makes sense.

This is the way to true charity and the remembrance of our equality as lights, or minds, and the makers of storytellers as well. It is in mastering the lesson of meeting others' fearful insistence *without* our own fearful resistance, that we honor them, ourselves, and, above all else, peace of mind. To see the outwardly disturbed through the eyes of wisdom is to see them as acting on their own inner devastation, going beyond effects and recognizing their cause. Then the situation can be dealt with rationally, with us willingly becoming the friend we would most want to meet if we were in such dire straits. Through this generosity to one who seemed to be both "other" and different, we learn that to be deluded by sensory perceptions and the storyteller's propaganda is a decision, not a disease. And that to stick up for everyone, and not just side with the few, is the reversal of fortune we have been seeking for in separate interests where it is not. And so now, here, where children believe in the impossible and adults disbelieve in the unreal, we see that we *all* deserve only what is good, not because of what is reasonable within, but because of what we are. Therefore, no credit is due anyone for what comes through us quite naturally, when we remember and get out of the way, no more than blame is due when we forget, all this leaving us thankful for the glimmering hope we actually *are* all that we could ever want to be.

THE SECOND FLOOR, PART III

As we've seen, the self-concept of the separated "me"—and its adjunct "and by the way, me first"—is no more than an image of a narcissistic narcosis, the seeming resident of a house constructed solely of smoke, mirrors, and shadows. And in the world of shadows alone does this idea of a separated personhood appear to be something other than the mind's imaginings. Here, where the story of the self "lives" out the storyteller's dread of all that calls into question its source in unbelief in the Possible, we who have identified with its story tremble in fear of exposure as well. And what makes this so absurd is that there is no occupant of the house of fog, our terror over the loss of what is made of gossamer threads and evanescent dust being the fear of losing what never was.

Yet, until we are free of all belief in the reality of the separated self and have escaped the corrupted thought system that attributes gain to the idea of selfishness, we must deal with its conflicted uprisings wherever they may occur. To meet fear, whether it manifests as greed or blamefulness toward others, with an inner quietness is the answer to what has absolutely no authority over the way we choose to think. Yet, we should not conclude that this will be an easy or quick fix to what is a deeply rooted problem; lulling ourselves into believing that because we've become more peaceful, others should too. Or that because we've decided to do better, our egoistic problems will simply disappear.

What needs to be transcended is the belief in neediness that claims we are bereft of any form of appreciation we cannot supply to ourselves. If we are not at rest and unmoved by the events that come and go in Storyland, we have chosen wrongly and are perceiving accordingly. Period. To free others from the storyteller's demands they behave in ways appropriate to the rules of its convoluted scripts is to escape the weird belief that the storyteller we made, made us. We are neither the images that flit about in Storyland, nor the storyteller telling us such stories of self. We are the minds, or lights, with the power to use all stories of the storyteller for the only reasonable purpose that exists: returning to sense and then waking up.

To be free of the suffocation of dependency is to recognize that if we need others, we don't love them; we need them. And that if we love others, we don't need them; we just love them. Accepting this will help us to see that, here on the second floor, it is our own strangling fingers that are wrapped around our throats, insisting always that our images be honored by others, who in turn demand we do the same. As stories, or bodies, we are in need in so many ways. As minds, or lights, we already have everything we need for comfort and assurance of worth. And once we are fully ensconced in the remembrance of that fact, the idea that we need others to be admiring or appreciative, or even civil for that matter, can be recognized for the foolishness it is. Another way to say this is that to live in want is to have an itch that cannot be scratched, and to realize what we really want is to no longer want at all is how the itch is made to disappear.

Do we need people for some things? Sure. Do we need others for moral support? Before and up to the reestablishment of our identification of ourselves with the atemporal mind, again, sure. After that, not really. Only when we stand completely independent of our psychological needs can we understand that we are strong. At that point, we are lights unto ourselves and, thereby, free of the darkness of our wrong-minded needs, doubts, and anxieties. Here we can stop pestering others to think as we do or act as we wish, aware that the key problem we face is never related to what the body, or story, gets or does not get, but our mistaken identification with these disappearing things as what we are.

What we find hard to accept is that every story, or body, our own fully included, is no more than an empty shell strutting around and around in the parade of personal pride, the mind behind all this nonsense accomplishing nothing of merit until it gives serious consideration to the idea that this may be a dream, and it may not be the character within it. In a practical sense, this would translate into the idea that there are always two worlds available for our viewing: one reflecting inclusion and truth; the other, the shadows of a separative lie. Body or mind, story or light, competitive or cooperative, which do we prefer? The world of differences as reality, or the acceptance of the idea that this world really *is* a Storyland we've all made up?

When a direct route is too threatening, an indirect and more circuitous route becomes the direct one, our wandering off being our way of strengthening ourselves to return once again. It takes time to realize that judgment and righteousness are handy minions of a fraud, defenses of a seeming specialness contradicting the thought that under our costumes—bodies, personalities, histories—we are one and all the same. In that chosen, but forgotten, state of denial, we peer about in Storyland, blinded by our ambitions, but still believing we see. Yet the light beyond the darkness we invented still shines serenely, awaiting our willingness to dismiss what we made in favor of what we are.

In the mirror of perception, one image "sees" another, unaware it is perceiving a picture of how it—unconsciously—sees itself. That is why the idea, "I don't really care what you think of me. I only care about what I think of you, because what I think of you will show me what I think of myself," is important. If we do indeed look in before we look out, the first question to pose ourselves is whether our thoughts and interpretations regarding what we perceive as reality are about authentic things or authored things. Only this healthy doubt has the power to lead us out of false certainty, the way to offer honest wonder to what is questionable at its very best.

What is fictional from the start cannot be turned into non-fiction by a fictional author, all of us the co-authors of one another's delusions, each as much a story as the stories "we" tell. In all our stories of self, shame and blame first looked at each other across an empty room, finding in the other exactly what it was seeking for in order to make itself seem real. These are the seeming opposites bestowing reality on one another, personal and projected accusations fostering belief in the unreal.

When the "heroic" within feeds like a vampire on the evil it has invented and perceives in the mirror to make itself seem true, its shrieks of accusation alone are enough to show clearly that the lady doth protest too much. Looked at closely, comparison and vanity are recognized as conjoined in a circle, the chicken and the egg story giving birth to a sense of self-importance that is induced and unreal. And only our resistance to hearing "we" are neither special nor real as separated selves keeps from our awareness that, beyond our fading costumes, we, who are not really different, are both permanent and safe, because we are not "we," but One. In more direct terms, when we truly smile again, it will be for the simple reason we have at last remembered *two is not true.*

In the story of the game in the icy river, it takes a while to accept that we retain the ability to look askance at any problem, no matter its size. The real problem is not what we usually believe is the real problem. The real problem is our buying into the small-minded thinking that insists this trial, whatever it may be, cannot be converted into a lesson in personal power; that it must remain as we've first seen it: something both quite disturbing and unjust. Yet the reality of the illusion of Storyland, as previously explained, is that the multitudinous and multifarious apparitions that seem to dictate our feelings and evoke our emotions have no more power to move us than that which we attribute to them. Seeing this, the question becomes why continue paying tribute to them at all?

If you or I were in bed dreaming, and aware we were dreaming, when a dream figure said "Boo!" to us, we'd

.nile at the thought. Well, since the story of our lives in Storyland is really no more than a story, here too, when another story, or body, or an unexpected event, says "Boo!" to us, the appropriate inner response is that same silent smile in return. What we should try to stay aware of is that the bacchanalia in the mind's cellar is like a Halloween party run amok. Here are the thoughts that seek to influence all aspects of the game that are played out on the first floor. Yet, no matter how often the bacchanalia's poison feeds into the main story, it has no power to make us drink from its cup.

"But something terrible just happened," we may say. So? Something terrible is always happening in the game, because the game of "I am more important than you" is, no matter its sometimes pretty covers, a terrible game. And if its frequent "boos" make us want to react with "boo-hoos," that is only because we've again lost sight of the fact that windmills of any size serve the purpose of hiding the fact there is no dragon, that we've forgotten we are the ones with the indomitable strength.

The reality of the world is that the Don Quixotes of Storyland, with their rusty spears, are contending only with shadows, no longer aware that anything less than a respectful approach to equals is not only undignified, but unworthy of what we truly are. To the thoughtful person on the second floor, the division of interests inherent in the game makes no sense, no more do we as we blithely go about our personal affairs, seeking our own advantage amidst the game's madness and chaos. On the first floor, we hope and wish for what we may never, and perhaps shouldn't, have. We insist we be glorified as persons and have only an occasional understanding that the purpose of the day is the healing of our minds, not the improvement of the seeming status of our stories, or bodies. We each seek respect for the image we've invented, but it can never be truly respected by anyone, ourselves included, for the very simple reason that *it is not real.* And to the same degree that hearing it is all made up strikes fear in our hearts, we have a certain witness to our continuing investment in the idea of being on our own as a separated self.

Yet made up or not, it still is necessary that we face the ugliness of our mistakes and the pain associated with them, if we are to go through the darkness of our guilt and our grief. Stepping out of denial of responsibility and its accusations of others, we learn that the real problem always was and is in our minds, in our choice to preserve the interests of the "me" we love, rather than seeing others' interests as just as important as our own. This is also how we learn that clinging to the past serves only the purpose of self-preservation and that, since our mistakes were made only in ignorance and error, *all* our supposed faults are unreal and not true. Once those mistakes have been understood not as crimes but mistakes we are sincerely sorry for, they are over and done. So why do we cling to them as if they were still here? Could it be that they suit the aim of giving support to the story of "me," our continuing guilt being the irrevocable "proof" that our sinfulness and, therefore, our supposed self must be true?

Despite the evidence constantly being provided by our minds' puerile self-slanders, we are not evil-doers caught in the snare of our errors, but confused minds whose every guilty thought is merely another facet of the trap woven of lies that is without any real power to keep us bound. And what is the answer to all this but to learn the not-so-easy-to-master lesson of quietly watching the fulminations of our egos and the appearances of bad memories with a healthy doubt about the veracity of *all* such hateful formulations of misthought?

Why is it so important to develop a healthy doubt about every memory as it arises? Memories are like library books, fictional tales about a past long over, kept seemingly real only by our bad habit of taking them out and reading—really writing—them again and again. To find ourselves re-reading book number 435, where someone betrayed us, or book number 789, another one of our stories of a shameful mistake we have already owned up to and apologized for, calls for no more than closing the book and returning it to the dustbin of our invented history from whence it came. Once we recognize this "self"-preserving, yet self-punishing, penchant for reaching for library books of this sort, and then tormenting ourselves with ghost stories for the masochistic activity it is, then perhaps, even though it will be harder than quitting smoking, for example, we will begin the process of reversal. And if we find ourselves unwilling to accept that the *only* thing that sustains our guilt is our belief in it—it having *no* other cause—and also unwilling to cease review-ing what, outside our imaginations, never was, at least we'll know that we, as the minds behind the storytellers, are complicit in the plot to make the dark tales of the self made of smoke and mirrors seem real.

Declaring the library vacant of value and closed, wanting to learn about the way our minds work from everything that happens, and welcoming all who come as equals require relinquishing our foolish habit of thinking that, because of our "vast experience" and "special gift of discernment," we know best. Only as we give up the insecurity of our need to be heard, and the uncertainty of our desire to be followed, can we recognize the opinions of others as equal to our own. Thus we can begin to learn we are not our opinions, a giant step toward learning we are neither the opinion-maker—nor really its defender.

Will we sometimes find ourselves in the position of pointing out to people that what they are doing is self-destructive? Or telling people in our zones of responsibility what to do and then expecting them to do it? Of course. But outside that, unasked, should we go around telling siblings, grown children, functional parents, friends, or others that they must do this or stop doing that? Not if we understand the real problem is not understanding that what makes us afraid is thinking we are superior, and what reminds us we are safe is remembering that while in illusions we appear different, in truth, we are one and all equals and, therefore, the same. The acceptance of this will save us from the sordidness of the specialness that says "I know better" and implies "I *am* better"—aspects of wrong-minded self-approval, the greatest trap of all.

To put what we really know in perspective, consider the vastness of the universe of universes, the almost countless galaxies and stars and all the unknown planets, the short history of civilization on earth, our own brief lives, and how much we really know about our great-great grandfathers, and where, or what, they may be now. Or where or what we ourselves may be a thousand years from now. And then, with an increased sense of humility, should we not in honesty say, "My goodness, since I know *so very little*, perhaps in relationships I should become one who is seen, but with a diminishing investment in the belief I should be heard"? We have a function of finding the truth of a shared inclusiveness, and telling others how they should live will not help us remember that function, while putting aside the desire to do so will.

What this means is that if we continue to think we have the wisdom to pontificate to others about what they best do, we should remind ourselves again and again of how little we really know. The fact is that we are all students in a classroom teaching *one* lesson: waking up to how abysmally we are treating some of our classmates in the stupefying tale of "how important I am," and out of the bleak story of separation from unity and each other as real. In this most important course of learning, paying close attention to the activity of our minds is essential, looking down in silence on all hateful thinking and negative memories being how we learn they are all concoctions of the storyteller designed to keep us immersed in the belief that its stories of self are what we actually are.

A better understanding of Storyland begins with accepting the thought that, because our perceptions and the banks of information from which they proceed are so limited in scope as to be basically insignificant, perhaps the final lesson to be learned is that we'll never truly understand more than that we don't understand. However, since the world of the game is such an inexplicable mess, maybe the idea that it is not understandable and cannot be explained is the very best news we could possibly receive. With this as a fresh starting point, and the realization we are students of the mind to support us, we can also see that it is good, not bad, that the trash in our minds—the supercilious sense of exasperation with others, the envy, our feelings of being put upon, of being unappreciated, and so on—comes into our conscious awareness. How else can we disown all of it, assuring ourselves it is neither of us nor anything we would ever want?

When we become unafraid enough to look at the arisings of our buried hostility without censorship and at things that go on in the cruel game with honesty, we will—because we are no longer defending—be able to see through and beyond them both. With this, we will be better able to consider the idea discussed earlier that if only what is eternal should be deemed to be true, then everything else must be, by the same definition, untrue. This would make not only us as we know ourselves, i.e., as bodies or stories of "I am separate, important, and real," but also the earth and the sun and the stars up above all part of a slowly disappearing fable—first us; eventually, all else as well. To look at things as they are is to see that what we call "time" is but the continuous ticking away of the ever-present and always fearful question, "How long am I going to last?" And yet, deep within and beneath the underlying anxiety that bubbles up to the surface of our minds, there is a stillness in which we realize that what we are is neither disappearing nor in the unbelief, and so we have no reason to fear or need to get out, because what we truly are has never been in.

To reiterate, we are lights, or minds, and our real objective is not personal gain, but to see through the storyteller's trickery. In Storyland, people beat their breasts in exultation or remorse, as though there were a real difference in swings of emotion over victories and losses that *both* serve the purpose of making our images seem real. They are equally deceptions, unmindful reactions to chance events in fantastical tales of separated selves that are apparent, but not true. This could be recognized and kept in awareness, but we are afraid of it, because it calls into question all we believe and think we know. And who would we be without all our seeming certainty?

Once we begin to suspect that Storyland is no more than a hoax, compassion for everyone—ourselves included—caught in the painful trap becomes not just charitable, but indisputably just and fair. To be just is to realize that those who are struggling with grief over what they believe they've done in falling in love with their stories, and whose eyes are covered over with frozen tears, cannot be expected to see before they can see. Only when they become ready will they be able to perceive their vainglorious descent into a separated self as a myth. Until then, they deserve nothing less than understanding in consideration of their plight—as, by the way, to repeat, do we when we forget our purpose and stumble and fall.

People wandering in the dark forest of isolation and all their perceived, and yet illusory, needs for affirmation and praise are, at times, self-centered and inconsiderate, not because they are evil, but because they are lost. And unless we make a sincere effort to see their untoward behaviors as the evident witnesses to their own tormented minds they must be and are, even if our behavior is more socially acceptable at the moment, we are just as lost as are they. To criticize those who don't understand is akin to belittling a blind person because he or she cannot see. If someone, at present, has no real concern about others, beyond how they can best serve his or her needs, it is simply because that person has lost sight of the benefits that come with keeping in awareness the equality that keeps us safe. In other words, when we use others' lack of understanding as justification to attack their way of being, we, too, are ignorant and frightening ourselves.

It bears repeating that anytime others are unfriendly or unkind, it is not because of our inadequacies or due to our mistakes, but only because at that moment they are unknowing, insecure, and afraid. Those who are offended by our errors *want* to be offended, otherwise they would be understanding, benevolent, and kind. And when we mimic their misbehavior and respond to their mistakes with defensiveness, it is only because at that moment we, too, are unknowing, insecure, and afraid. If we could perceive properly, we would recognize *every* argument we enter into as no more respectable than two cats hissing and spitting at each other in an alley. Fighting with others over what, in the long run, doesn't matter much at all may serve to make our conflicted stories of self seem real for a while longer, but it does nothing toward helping us to remember that, under these Halloween costumes, there are no true differences among those who are equal.

How incredibly mistaken—in source, expression, and outcome—is our entering into any form of conflict with equal lights because they have forgotten who they are and made mistakes. This doesn't mean that we don't defend ourselves in a normal sense. But it does suggest that when someone appears to be the cause of our distress, we might try to picture a bridge in our minds between the upset we are experiencing, where we seem to be, and peace of mind. With the help of such a picture, it would be possible to consider something not usually conceivable: that it could actually be our fear of crossing that bridge, and not the other person or the situation, that is the "reason" behind our feeling so distraught. Everyone still attached to the belief in self-importance fears crossing the bridge from the desert of selfishness to the oasis of shared interests. For when we are in that oasis, situations, even those that are fraught with difficulty, are no longer given the power to sweep us away. And this makes the storyteller tremble, because if we were constantly bothered by nothing and no one, who would be left to be taken in by all its agitation and seriousness?

Another thing to try to keep in mind is how counterproductive it is to continue displacing our inner problems with choice outside of our minds onto others and situations where they cannot be solved. And to see that we do this because we don't want them, like the storyteller, solved, their resolution opening the way to living a life in which there is no seriousness and no excitement, only the continual calmness of light. And so in place of this quietness, we choose to remain *non compos mentis*, minds without a country, accepting a beggarly notion of an always needy self as better than having no self at all. Let's see, a conflicted image of self requiring constant defense, appreciation, and attention, or a peaceful state of mind in which, as lights, we need nothing to be different in order to remain at rest. I wonder which we should devote ourselves to.

A helpful way to think of this is that when we become upset because of the mistakes others are making in their lives, what we don't see is that we are still secretly accusing ourselves of the same. Those who have faced the results of their ignorance and forgiven themselves no longer see reason to condemn anyone. When we judge others and accuse them of betrayal of their responsibilities, we separate ourselves from them, unaware we are continuing in the belief we have broken our promise to remain one with our Self who encompasses all. This unconscious fear that says we are guilty is why we project, and what we are afraid to look upon, not because we believe it is true, but—since it would mean the end of us as we have come to believe we are—because we sense it is not. We have *not* broken away from unity because, being an integral part of the Self, we could not, and cannot, depart from what we are. And so our fears of retribution or oblivion are meaningless, understood better as we cease to condemn in exchange for the single message to all who are lost: "You have *not* done what you think and feel secretly ashamed of; you have *not* betrayed your sacred trust."

When we are outside the sphere of influence of our self-centeredness, we want the same thing for everyone as for ourselves: the very best. When we are caught up in the drama of the storyteller's self-adoring self, we want things to be better for ourselves even if that just means that they be worse for others. Each desire shows our alignment, or lack thereof, with reason and the idea of goodwill toward all, the embrace of which alone leads us out of the guilt that comes in the wake of selfishness. That the cruel game in the icy river is based on the idea of "me first" is undeniable. That the fulfillment of our "me first" desires rewards the winners with prizes fraught with dissatisfaction is equally beyond question, the stories of the world speaking to us in the tongues in which we have spoken to them.

When we become perturbed because someone has treated us dismissively, or in some other way seemingly disregarded or degraded us, we have abandoned the certainty found in the oasis of calm, crossing the bridge back into the realm lit only by the insecure and flickering lamplights of pride. And because we have reentered the dark vale of vanity, we again see not at all, the other's mistakes becoming personal and insulting at best, unreasonable affronts to the image we have made and must always protect. And thus we find our "justifications" for separating into unjustifiable wars, the betrayal of unity and the Self that no one pretending to be the "good" victim of a "bad" victimizer can afford to see for what it is.

We cannot deny what we see in Storyland, but we can and must learn to deny that our misperceptions of what we see have the power to make us dance to their fitful tunes. Our goal is to learn to be truly quiet at all times, in a state of equanimity even when our stories, or bodies, are in the most challenging of circumstances. The world of denial of the Possible changes from a penal colony to a classroom the moment we make the decision to use everything that occurs in it to help remind us that the meaning we find in it comes solely from us. A sense of cheerfulness born of trust in our ability to cope with *anything* is the real prosperity we seek, all states other than peace of mind being forms of agitation and nothing else.

And so, as we leave the second floor, we can begin to appreciate that while many books may have been read and lectures listened to or attended, the real lesson is that the teacher and the student are within and are one. And what is to be learned but that in everyone we perceive, we look on either fellow students and equal lights or judgmental imaginings in stories of our own making: one or the other, in the reflection of our choice? And with this learning to guide us, when each person we meet becomes to us, at the moment, the most important person in the universe, we will know that we have returned to reason and have found the promise of peace in the simple idea of seeing beyond differences in form to the bright hope of finding everyone the same.

THE THIRD FLOOR, PART I

The move to the third floor comes with doing our best to live with the idea that the *only* honest thought we can hold about our stories is that they are all made up and, therefore, taken seriously, are misleading in the extreme. What makes this particularly difficult to accept is that it represents the undoing of our belief in an objective reality, along with the relinquishment of our cherished power to accurately assess and judge. In the cruel game of special-ness in the icy river, people live by judgment and die to sameness, many dividing themselves off into what they have determined to be exclusive and, for some, even "holy" separations. Yet the exclusion of equals and judgment of those who are alike are just more forms of murderousness played out in this very strange world where people are born with the sole certitude that eventually they must die.

As we've seen, every mind believing it is a fictional character here in Storyland has a version of reality it projects onto the world. Together, they let their sleepiness and their senses and their interpretations convince them their histories of self are not just stories, but things that are real and significant and true. Thus, their lives in Storyland become to them not only important, but sacred. Yet, in reality, none of us have *anything* in common with these shabby fictions we have for too long been taking ourselves to be. And while this thought will likely initially frighten us in our worry over the loss of self, it will make us supremely grateful when we realize this means the abolition of our wrong-minded belief in guilt and dismissal of all the despair that has followed in its deadly wake.

Once we understand we are living in our own made-up versions of reality, the idea of being free to select better versions begins to make sense. Very difficult situations can be seen as offering us the gift of reconsideration of what we had been convinced was both factual and causative in favor of accepting that how we feel comes from our minds and *not* the situation at all. Now, with the help of this greater insight, a coworker or boss can be seen as someone expressing his or her inner pain over a grief that has neither cause nor logical antecedent. At the same time, with the aid of a new perception of the other as sad, not bad, our desire to be nasty in return has that much less power to seduce. And in refusing that temptation to attack we can, as said earlier, look beyond to the realization that if we find ourselves holding something against another, it's evidence we are still holding something against ourselves. For if we were holding nothing against ourselves, it would be impossible for us to hold anything against anyone— ever.

Through the process of coming to recognize grievances as defenses of the unbelief and setting them aside, we can start to understand that offering anything less than genuine compassion to the bereft is actually assaultive, not only to the other, but ourselves as well. And so we find in every situation good reason to be generous to all. However, until we are free from the final vestiges of self-importance, our progress will be intermittent, meaning there will be times of relapse when we forget our purpose is to be kind. But what is that to us who can quickly recall ourselves to that purpose, and, in the cathedral of light of the present hour, begin a life of generosity again?

Talking about the sanctuary of the cathedral of light of the present hour is not just "happy talk," but rather a way of describing a place of refuge and protection bounded by trust and confidence, an hour of oasis set apart in the great dark desert of time past and future. It is in the honesty of taking responsibility for what we perceive and how we react that the means to our goal is recognized and accepted. If we are the power behind the storyteller, offering its stories all the belief or disbelief they end up with and have, then no matter their size, scope, or attributes, nothing whatsoever is up to stories at all. This is the understanding that leads to a new interpretation of relationships, freeing us of the chains of a seeming external oppression we unknowingly labored under heretofore.

When we become aware that beyond their—bleak or bright—costumes others are really minds, or lights, one and the same and our closest kin, we will look on them and their behaviors differently. The proper perception of those who play the selfish game of "me first," which includes *everyone* until he or she gets fed up enough to start to swim for the shore, is that they feel lonely and deprived because they are wandering in circles in darkness. And, as was said before, what are people who are lost and acting up really looking for but just one person who is sensible enough to be defenseless, silently asking everyone they meet, "Will *you* be the rational one I've been desperately seeking?"

It is not really a case of *can* we hear those who call out for a friend, but *will* we hear them? To cross the bridge into silence is frightening only to the constantly noisy "me," our identification with the same made real only through our desire and sufferance. We're no more these stories of self than we are the man in the moon. But that most of us are—more or less—clinging to the concept of wanting to be more than stories is demonstrated by our anger, our guilt, our worries, and our blame. Yet, despite all these continuing problems in identification, we truly remain as innocent as we were and could ever wish to be.

In our stories of self, we have betrayed our common ancestry and wholeness, buying into the storyteller's thought system of how we are apart and, therefore, must be different. But what seems to have been accomplished in fictional stories is merely fictional. And so in Truth, where everything is beyond question and nothing is left to chance, nothing has happened and there is no ground to be repaired. Our seemingly serious serial stories of special-ness are no more than the detritus of confusion, fallen cobwebs of fertile imaginations, there only to be swept away. We cannot really be apart or away from a Self that is all there is, the story of self—body, personality, and history—separate from the "I Am That I Am" having no more substance than a wisp of fog being met by the morning sun. Despite the terrible things we see and hear and remember in our spellbound condition, the *only* real state is one of absolute perfection, *all* other states no more than witnesses to the self-convincing lie we have repeated to ourselves and told all else who would listen.

If we find it hard to believe that this is all make-believe, it is not because it is so hard to accept—how hard can it be to become unconvinced of the reality of a world filled with death and a mind gripped by guilt and fear?—but because we want to be the "I am" we've made and still cherish too much to let go. Yet, when we finally take off our invented image and hang it on the wall like a no-longer-useful suit of armor, when people come either to gaze at it in admiration or to vilify it in whatever way, we will be unencumbered by the odd notions that accompanied it, now aware they are reacting to no more than their own projections of meaning onto an empty shell. And then flattery and insult will be acknowledged as related to an image and, therefore, in our new estimation, regarded as of no worth.

If Storyland is totally a fiction, then the book in front of us, the hands holding it, and the eyes and the brain that appear to be doing the reading are all as much a part of the story as the book itself. And yet something is reading it and trying to make sense of its message that everything other than Truth is an illusion and means absolutely nothing at all. And what could that be other than the rational part of our minds using the vehicle of words and thoughts to reassure ourselves that nothing untoward has happened because nothing untoward *can* happen, and that "coming home" means nothing more than releasing our grip on what is impossible, and that, only at the speed at which we so choose?

On the third floor, we begin to realize that setting our images aside is a necessary prerequisite for "coming home," achieved through learning that it is only because we have not wanted real freedom we are unaware we are free. If everything we experience has the potential to benefit us, e.g., difficult circumstances and trying people aiding us in remembering we are minds that choose our attitudes, then what could the real purpose of stories in the cruel game of clashing images be but to help us realize that something as vicious as your interests in competition with mine must be part of a nightmare? And that from nightmares recognized as such, the only sensible reaction would be to awaken and arise?

In the strange shell game of "look at how important I am," the process of awakening is one of self-observation, of watching our conditioning and its responses to the stories of self in order to discover how attached we are to the absurd and the inane. "Yes, that's all well and good," we may say, "but this one did that, and that one is saying this, and they are both very mean, and what they do hurts so bad." True, if we are vulnerable bodies, or stories. Otherwise, says who? Says only the conditioning we've developed over time and now give the right to posture as reasonable. However, because it actually makes no sense, when we listen to its interpretations of reality, we are wrong! Not in what the other is doing or saying, but in the self-deceiving thought that anyone or anything in an untrue story has the power to Shanghai us away from the oasis of peace within.

Remembered yet or not, equanimity in all circumstances is our natural state; complete patience with everyone and about everything the reasonable response to a place of fiction that is just that and nothing more. Yet, when we are still so caught up with the first-floor idea of everything being about winning and losing, it is very difficult to see how illogical it is to have an investment in a zero-sum game where every gift is a deceptive trinket with a patina of gloss disguising the fact it has no value to be sought or found. In the calm and quiet oasis, there is neither excitement nor despair, because there is no separated self to be defended or made to feel guilty. And so, there is no further attraction to the allure of suffering and sorrow, their calls to self-pity unwanted and, in time, undone.

When we set to the side and go beyond the storyteller's fear of stillness, it becomes more and more apparent that the end of the story of self comes with the realization it had no true beginning and, therefore, outside our wishes that it exist, no reality as well. A temporary and seeming existence, which is all the "I am important—and often insulted" has, is an epithetic and fleeting illusion and nothing else. And yet, we must not underestimate our entrancement with either it or with blame as a way out of our pain. It is very difficult to accept that what we've been in love with is nothing, or that our feelings of anger and annoyance are not what they appear, but defenses of the ephemeral. Hard, too, is it to avoid lingering in the storyteller's lair of shame once we've recognized that what we have been blaming others for we've been doing to ourselves.

In the great School of Reconciliation with Reason, as we go beyond our fear over the loss of self to the state of recognizing *everyone* as a mind, or a light, and alike and the same, we can start to accept the absolute meaninglessness of *every* story of separation and specialness we've told ourselves, remember, or perceive. The projected stories we see are no less than hypnotic blocks to sight and understanding, but only for as long as we give them permission to be. As we become less beguiled by our judgments and "understanding," and more capable of perceiving that everything in the strange tea party we are at is to us actually neutral until we engage with it, we will realize that to *everyone* and *everything* we are saying, "This is what I want you to be in your influence on me." The game in the icy river takes place in the land of the blind, where the truly sensible person who opens one eye and sees it for what it is no longer wants to be ruler, as he or she did when still blind, but only wishes to awaken from what is now perceived as a nightmare without all hope of redemption from within.

THE THIRD FLOOR, PART II

Every game in the world, taken seriously, is a distraction and a defense against realizing that nothing in Storyland is serious. There is no truth in any lie, and Storyland is a lie, an empty fiction given form. And so our real journey is not one of self-improvement, but within, to find again what could never be lost and, therefore, cannot be found. Yet, because it cannot be lost does not mean it cannot be forgotten, which obviously it has been, but also that it can, and sooner or later cannot fail to, be remembered by all. This, in turn, calls for changing nothing, as, in an honest appraisal of worth, we slowly come to the rejection of all else for the simple reason it fails to satisfy.

As we become more aware that the sights we perceive and assign meaning to are like snippets cut randomly from a ponderous, profane, and utterly senseless cloth, we'll become less enamored of the flickering and passing, and better prepared to seek elsewhere for stability and peace of mind. The virulent states of self-exaltation and its concomitant grief everyone seemingly here experiences are the result of a pernicious entrancement by a master magician whose hidden name is "us." Glee over getting one's way is a noxious weed pretending to be a bouquet of flowers; sorrow over what appears to be failure, under its somber garments, an insidious appeal to enter into self-pity— equally unhelpful to one trying to learn what is really taking place in the minds of the inhabitants of the land of the frightened and not free.

The mind that gives credence to the storyteller's tales or decides to reject them all is the real puppeteer; the restless churning of a thought system based on separation and self-making best met with a silent observation and no opposition at all. And if we do just that, meaning sit back and quietly watch the mind's activities, what do we see? "You should have…." "You shouldn't have…." "I should have…." "I shouldn't have…." "He should have…." "She shouldn't have…." "What if…?" "I really want…." "I wish I had…." "I wish I hadn't…." "I sure hope…." "Why did I…?" "Why didn't I…?" "Why did they…?" "Why don't I…?" "Why should I…?" "I can't stand him…." "I hate that…." "Why me…?" And on and on the stream of thought without enough information for us to make a wise decision takes its ill-advised course, all the while seeking to drag us into its river of mud, succeeding whenever we are gullible enough to fall for its guile instead of simply watching it go by.

This nonsensical "thinking" provides the foundational "logic" behind a storybook world. And once we see this self-fabricated mess from its original premise of division into duality as beneficial for what it is, we'll soon realize that the answer is not to straighten it out, but to let it go. Something with its source in conflict cannot be made peaceful no matter how we work to make it so. While we are clearly two or more in our stories of multiplicity, under the covers of our Halloween costumes, in reality we remain as we were: One.

If we were to line up in our minds the President, the Prime Minister, the Pope, a peon, and a pauper, and lay their costumes, our stories about them, and their bodies down in our sight, behind each one we would find a light. If we were to then line up in our minds our wives or husbands, our mothers or fathers, our daughters or sons, our sisters or brothers, our aunts or uncles, and lay their costumes, our stories about them, and their bodies down in our sight, behind each of them we would find exactly the same light we found behind the President, the Prime Minister, the Pope, the peon, and the pauper. Then, as we became ready, we could generalize this idea and transfer this vision of equal lights to everyone we've ever known or seen, friends and "enemies" alike, and to everyone else we may know or see or even hear of from this moment on. And when we've at last, not only willingly, but gladly, completed this assignment, we will also recognize this light seen in all as a symbol of the light of Truth, or our Self. And that, because it is in everyone without exception, it therefore must be the only truth in us as well.

This is the purpose we can give to Storyland: to learn through charity, understanding, forgiveness, and honesty to see again right here where once we were blind—to offer welcome to our Self in every encounter, be that meeting in the world or in our minds. And, in that, to learn to dismiss the seeming reality of every judgment that stands in the way of the glad welcome our Self holds out to each and all of us as One.

This projected world of confusion is populated by a host of illusions going on and on about things that change and go bump in the night. And this is what passes as truth until the minds behind the apparitions begin to recognize the nothingness of it all, the storytellers of tall tales most fully included. The reason behind our seeming to be here, where conflict rules the day, is not to seek to satisfy the ever-increasing appetite of self-aggrandizement. Rather it is to learn it is both possible and sensible to return to the quiet place in our minds beyond the chaos without and the idle chatter within that accompanies it. For it is silence alone that truly speaks, all else being the noise of shutters rattling in the wind.

As we become wiser about what is going on in our minds, we can see that there cannot be feelings of betrayal without expectation, or expectation without a hidden wish for the disappointment that makes us, as stories, seem real and the storyteller safe. And so it is not really people or circumstances we must learn to be patient with, but the thoughts of bitterness and complaint in our minds. It is watching without judgment that will naturally lead us to doubt their reality. Because the world believes in separation and blame, and many people we know are caught up in these beliefs, doesn't mean we are compelled to go along with what, looked upon judiciously, is counterproductive at best. If we were to raise ourselves up out of our ill-conceived pursuits in a madhouse and say, "This is insane," we might fear the loss of companionship of those who don't think the same. But once we understand what the power of our disbelief has accomplished, we will realize that only in the game of separation and opposition are we truly lonely and alone.

The way out of the fear of disappearance that accompanies such loneliness is to give away all thought of our supposed needs and learn to die—before we die—to our identification with what, without our support, has no choice but to fade away. Undoing our belief in what we are not is the only accomplishment worthy of note. Succeeding at the game while failing at this makes all our worldly accomplishments misconstrued achievements at best. There is no doubt we can find ourselves self-satisfied, or even delighted, when we succeed at something in the game. Nor should we cease our efforts to do well, or repress our feelings when we do. But we certainly should begin to ask ourselves, *what* is so pleased that it got its own way? And ask ourselves, why would we want a way to get when that so plainly means there is a way to lose and become disappointed about as well? Wouldn't learning how to be at peace with whatever comes, and therefore is, be more rational? Yet, we might find ourselves asking, "Who would I be without all that I look forward to?" Perhaps someone who has found complete, absolute, and unperturbed patience with the passing a far greater gift than any enchantment of the game—a sensible person who doesn't believe in the reality of ghost stories any longer.

It should give us pause to think there is reality to a world where "love" can turn to hate for reasons as insubstantial as (needy) advances being rebuffed or (seeming) affection unrequited. If we become truly balanced, will we be all that concerned with what are plainly egocentric needs? Or with what people say about an "us" they are making up in their minds out of their imaginations and thin air? Or even with what our own wrong-minded judgments and comparisons are going on and on about?

If true contentment can be found *only* in a peaceful state of mind, all else must be leading us unwittingly to despair. Yet, if we grow in our ability to meet our upsets with everyone more calmly, upset itself will be seen for the quicksand it is. With this, the reality of our upset with others can be understood as merely a denial we are in the same quicksand they're in. If we will trace people who seem to be disturbing to us back to their country of origin, we'll discover they were born in our minds. And what applies to people applies to circumstances as well. As dark thoughts disappear in the light of silent watching, so upset loses its steam in a responsible admission of what we've been up to and doing to ourselves.

To summarize, we are minds giving support to the storytellers we've allowed to convince us we are bodies, or stories, and to clear up that confusion is our immediate task. What greater confusion could there be than to believe we are what we are not, and not to believe we are what we are? This is the source of all our other confusions. And until it is clarified, we remain certain to be confused. Yet, even while drowning in self-concern in the game in the icy river, we can grow in faith that closing our eyes doesn't mean that the light has left. This is the light shining forever beyond all passing stories and storytellers in minds that are self-deceived and nothing worse than that. In the kindly sight of eternal gentleness, our mistakes are understood as the result of ignorance alone—true forgiveness for mistakes made in a lack of understanding freeing all from the terrible and yet delusional burden of guilt.

THE THIRD FLOOR, PART III

As we examine what is going on in the game from a deeper perspective, we can see that there is no such thing as evolution in a scene shifted about within its own frame, but never changed in content. For while a number of people in Storyland have become more sophisticated and adept at self-deception, all that means is that the savage nature of our self-centeredness has been made more obscure and, therefore, more difficult to discern and deal with. Uncovering and uprooting this pernicious thinking is a prerequisite for coming back into accord with the unspoken language of Truth.

The undoing of the dark desire to be a special, spoiled, and seeming self of great worth brings with it the absolution of the belief in sin and dissolution of the idea we are hostages of karma. As we've seen, behind every story of self-importance, there is an unknowing mind caught up in the tall tale the storyteller is telling. Within this alien condition, the mind sees what it wants to see, hears what it wants to hear, thinks what it chooses to think, reacting to its own interpretations of meaning without any real idea of what it is doing. This mesmerized mind is ours, leaving our only productive function in this place of constant affliction, lit by the smoking torchlights of our slyness and competitiveness, to come out of our self-hypnosis in peace. With this higher aspiration to sustain us, we can begin to grow in awareness that since light is not subject to either approach or alteration by darkness, as the lights we actually are, neither are we.

The game of contention in the icy river is fundamentally disturbing, because in it we are feeding the self-centeredness we hold dear instead of defending the rights and equality of all. When people fight over religion or what they call "the truth," they are engaged in nothing other than a war of uncertainty and personal opinions. Thus, when we ourselves enter into any of these bitter contests of beliefs we assert are important, and then think we have to defend in what we see as a game of survival, we end up feeling guilty. And this, because deep inside we know that fighting is always an attempt to dominate another, and that domination is like theft from the common good, and just as plainly ugly and wrong. In simple terms, when we think meanly or act badly and want to continue in that vein, we are no longer in alignment with what is good and true, and when we are in that condition of mind, we *must* end up unhappy, because we are out of alignment with what we are.

Either *everything* on this side of the curtain of amnesia, or unbelief in the Possible, is real and the idea of the light on the other side is a myth, or light is the symbol for the ineffable and everything here is a fable, with no compromise possible between the two. For lights, or minds, the lesson is that peace and happiness are exactly the same, and turning in that direction is the only thing that makes sense. Among the first steps in that direction is to ask ourselves what the world might look like without the interference of our projections and prejudices to darken what is there. If we removed these malformed impressions made solely by our imaginations, would it not dawn on us they were merely appearances that, beyond what we wanted them to stand for, actually stood for nothing at all?

As recovery of the awareness of reason is concomitant with a diminishing belief in the reality of senselessness, so release from the narcissistic trap we appear to be in comes with the growing realization we are not in the trap, just caught in self-convincing lies that insist we are. We can't, or at least we shouldn't, deny our bodies or our experiences. Yet we *should* ask ourselves, is it really possible that we, who are true, can be entrapped by the false? Is it likely that darkness can come near and then overlap the light? Is it reasonable to assume that we, who are in reality perfectly still, can be overcome by the amplified noise of tiny and meaningless thoughts worrying about a self that is not even there? The answer to these questions, and all others that arise to confound us, is that any place in which death seems to have the last word must be ridiculous from start to finish and, therefore, even though apparent, cannot be what it seems.

The end of belief in our stories as true is the end of belief that the storyteller has something of merit to say and the beginning appreciation of the idea that perhaps only silence has anything worthwhile to impart. Why do we put such an emphasis on what we think of as knowledge here in Storyland, when all our seeming understanding of what things mean is built on the foundation stone of the idea that "I am different and more important than you"? From such a doubtful basis, what can we possibly have learned that is reliable? If we gave all that confused cogitation up, might we find underneath it the true wisdom that would help us overcome our grief over a seemingly shameful past, so that we might come to recognize ourselves as untrammeled minds and not stories at all? Would not all other "overcoming" be trifling in comparison, since all other overcoming is of self-limits, yet still within the boundaries of a belief in the self? The self that "overcomes" itself is still only a self—separated and incapable of reaching beyond its limits to the unbounded stillness and purity of light.

As was said before, it is disbelief in darkness that leads to recognizing the light, which in turn leads to the awareness that if all others are lights, we must be as well. If embracing our stories of unworthiness has led us deeper into confusion, then accepting that all others, like us, are literally doing their best must be the way out of the shadowy prison house of conceit. When the ancient and rusty gates of blame and unforgiveness finally swing open, we will step through and into the freedom of pardon fully given and thus understood as fully received. Here on the third floor, we can recognize that the light is our own because we belong to the Light, the deeper doorway within opening to the remembrance of our ever-present Self; the path of safe return ours because we've at last accepted that it belongs to all.

THE FOURTH FLOOR, PART I

The fourth floor is the state of mind where it more fully enters our awareness that the purpose of learning is to reach to where we can trust enough to let our uncertain "certainty" go and return again to a truly open mind. What is real learning but to learn there is no learner; real wisdom but to remember that no one is wise other than our Self? If the wise are kind, and the kind alone are the wise, how wise are we? Is there more for us to learn? Further within for us to travel? Or are we still wedded to that strange spouse, the shabby belief that these stories of self, or bodies, or learners, is what and all we are? Honestly, are we?

In the same way that all of us are the same or none of us are the same, so all our stories are the same, or none of them are the same. Good stories, like bad stories, are bad stories when they lull us into believing that any story is good and not just nothing at all. Stories are just stories. Yet it takes time and trust and patience to assimilate new concepts such as, in a story that is incapable of producing real happiness, excitement is not helpful and disappointment is. Or to accept something as far out of accord with our prior thinking as "I am—you are, we are—not." Or to seriously consider the idea that *all* of time and space, Storyland writ large, is no more than a changing and slowly dissipating bad dream.

If the ineffable reality of Truth is best "described" as found in the perfect quietness of Self, then the self we made, along with every thought and belief and memory that accompanies it, is actually best "described" as simply one part of a large cloud of disappearing nonsense and nothing more. In looking with honesty at things as they are, it becomes apparent that humans, the animals, the earth, the sun, the moon, and the stars are, at their own pace, all vanishing into silence. It is the stillness behind the noise that denies we, who are lights, could ever be unfaithful to our trust, the fount of wisdom that gives new meaning to the actions we are so busily engaged in as we pass through these incomprehensible fictions of what it means to be real and, therefore, really alive.

As we look objectively at our precarious condition in the world of the "I am," we will realize that if "Storyland" is a valid description of where we seem to be, because it's where we've agreed to be, it must also be possible for us to disagree with anything and everything we've agreed to heretofore. This would mean that we can step out from under the sway of the storyteller's interpretations of reality at any time we choose, and that when we forget this is so, which, being deeply conditioned, we will for a while, we can pause long enough to remember we made the storyteller, meaning the storyteller did not make us.

As we begin to assume responsibility for sight and emotion, what real forgiveness of "others" is starts to become clearer. If it is our minds that choose to believe in the storyteller's version of reality, or not, then we are really the ones telling the body, or the story, what to think, or see, and how to feel about the perception. Therefore, from a psychological or emotional viewpoint, everyone is our own invited guest. Once we can accept that what we experience as external derives its meaning from our minds, and that we *are* those minds, we can understand we are not forgiving others for their misbehaviors, but ourselves for our lapses in vigilance and misinterpretations of what things really mean.

To repeat a central idea, the reality of interpersonal relationships is that we cannot be affronted—or bothered or made impatient or angered—by anyone's behavior or language, and that when we find ourselves so, we've done it to ourselves. In one sense, you might say that if we are finding another's act uncomfortable, it is because it is reminding us of what we have denied and do not want to see: that under the cloak of the disguise we've adopted, what we think we are is just an act too. Unfriendliness, aloofness, hostility, rejection, dismissiveness, ingratitude, and so forth on the part of the unwary, unknowing, and unseeing, perceived rightly, become opportunities to learn whether we've chosen to be under the influence of our wrong-mindedness, which sees all others as opponents, or have regained the understanding that no matter a person's present state of mind, everyone is actually a classmate and not an enemy in the game.

At the level of the state of mind termed the fourth floor, we become aware that the weird and inconsequent thinking of the storyteller has *nothing* to do with the stillness that comes with what we are. It is in quietness we recognize that to lose our self is to find our Self, slowly growing in the conviction that self-effacement is not destruction but discovery. It is in the process of dis-engaging from our engrossment with what we are inventing that we begin to think and act as though it's all just a fiction without either meaning or consequences. This is the learning that leads to the awareness that *perfect* forgiveness *must* mean forgiving what *never* happened at all.

To be told what we remember is a myth, and that all we see, hear, think, and are so sure of is no more than a chimera, or an illusion, is difficult to countenance. We may be living a hard life and question why someone or something has placed us in such difficult straits, but question the reality of our beliefs and even the authenticity of the sufferer? Rarely so. Yet, only thus can we become aware, as lovers of the "I am," and even more of the power we invented to tell ourselves stories and make them seem real, that we are secretly holding ourselves account-able for the impossible-to-accomplish-in-reality rejection of the Self. This rejection is what we feel guilty about and is the real source of the distress that we, in all of our projections and anger, are trying to blame others for having caused us. But since in truth we *are* the Self, the whole thing is ludicrous from beginning to end. No one is to blame for what could not happen and, therefore, did not happen. And yet we suffer over it. Not because it is real, but because we *must* suffer over it to make our fantasies of self and separation seem real. Otherwise, how could we be important and unique, standing beyond unity, with something of great meaning to convey?

The cleverness of the storyteller we gave power to seduce us into this quagmire must be recognized for what it is. It makes up a lurid tale of specialness it convinces us to buy into. It then pretends to apologize for what it hopes it has done and has the story it invented groan and weep over its "sins." Yet it is all secret worship at the reliquary of false power, a devious attempt by the storyteller to deflect attention from its own insubstantial nature by having the self it made pay a price in coins of guilt for what was completely impossible in Truth.

Thus the reality is that the self "outside" the Self exists only in the imagination of the imaginary storyteller—and in the mind that joins with it in belief, the story of the storyteller itself being no more than an invention as well. This means the real purpose of all study is to lead us to the conclusion that no matter how seemingly erudite our beloved "I am" may become, a story is still a story and has no reality at all. That nothing has happened to change our eternal unity within the Self, because nothing *could* happen to what never changes, means there is no lasting learner behind our studiousness and nowhere to go with our learning but beyond it to rest. This is how learning that repeats itself in more and more sophisticated forms finally disappears into not knowing, with the wisdom of silence replacing the accumulated "knowledge" that is, outside its helpfulness in awakening us to eternal quiet, ultimately not much more than noise.

THE FOURTH FLOOR, PART II

There is no doubt that it requires dedication and hard work to master the skill of watching the various forms of fear that rise up in our minds without either turning away or offering them credence. This is the way to the higher viewpoint from where we begin to perceive that things in an illusion are not a matter of good and bad, but of real or unreal, how we gain the understanding that all our darkened thoughts and negative memories are merely echoes of a call that was never made, that there was and is nothing and no one behind them.

As we shed the garments of delusion and self-centeredness and return to the awareness of our real kinship with everyone, we free ourselves to realize that those in the game acting cruelly are expressing their irrational subservience to wrong-mindedness, acting as minions of the lie. So why would we want to respond to them in kind, unless we, too, wanted to be part of that same corruption of true intent? What they are asking for in truth is for someone, anyone, to recognize their struggle for what it is and offer them the respect they, at the moment, are incapable of offering themselves. They ask for the same understanding we all want. And if we offer it to them when they are in need of it, we will discover it is ours. For example, if we were to offer our parents, be they dead or alive, the respect, consideration, kindness, and encouragement we wanted from them when we were young, we would realize we have all those qualities and, though we didn't know it back then, had no need to ask them of any special consideration at all.

To be steady in a refusal to judge or oppose the ways of equals is the way out of the thought system that insists differences of opinion have meaning, which, being only opinions, clearly they have not. This also means that striving to convert others to our ways of thinking merely demonstrates how insecure we really are. In fact, seeing ourselves—psychologically speaking—as needing anything from others we cannot supply to ourselves simply reinforces resentment over the idea that they have been given something we have not. Certainly, in Storyland, we all have different forms and talents. Yet equally certain is the fact that the more "talented" are not always better off than those who seem less attractive or gifted. For us, the lesson is that when we want—believe we need— something from another, we'll too often make ourselves subject to him or her and then behave in undignified ways.

When everything is understood as a lesson not in getting, but in waking up out of our comas of need, the dark desert of complaint made barren by envy is seen in a new light, because every classmate, nice or not, is there recognized as a friend. This more generous perception of equals will elevate our appreciation of life and give meaning to why we are here, which is to gradually become aware we are not. For as the pages of our stories of the past slowly turn blank in terms of meaning, we will realize that the authors of these cruel non sequiturs are as fictional as the tales of guilt they wrote and we so avidly read.

As lights are unified and, therefore, undifferentiated, so the character in the story and the storyteller are one. The belief in what does not exist and the believer in the same are the chicken and the egg: the belief producing the believer, and the believer confirming the belief. The conundrum of the chicken and the egg story is undone as we, who are neither a we nor a who, get over our perverse need to preserve both the storyteller and the self. *Real progress comes with our ceasing to take seriously the idea that there is someone who is unrealized or who needs to progress.* Once we see that progress comes with undoing, not doing, we can relax into the idea that "enlightenment" is ours the moment we accept there is no "I" to become enlightened. With this, "what's in it for me?" becomes transmuted into concern for everyone we meet, which in turn leads us out of the grim tyranny of self-importance and all our desperate attempts to make sense out of what cannot be understood.

To truly understand is to understand that there is nothing understandable on a vast plain of continually unfolding conflict, where friendship so often inexplicably turns into enmity, and nothing we see lasts or can be counted on in our travails. Are we to believe Storyland's history of centuries of wars is "understandable" or that there is reality to the sightings—or stories—of a man beating a horse, harpooning a whale, clubbing a seal, whipping arrows into a deer, shooting an elephant, or murdering a neighbor, or even our eating a hamburger or a carrot—truth to a dream wherein a part of what is One actually does harm to another?

In such an incomprehensible world, the only real gift we can give is to subtract our story from the larger one made from all our stories, withdrawing conviction from the shared delusion that something as bizarre as this disappearing world we inhabit could ever be more than a fiction. Here, where freedom from past and present judgments offered everyone becomes the gift we receive, all memories are seen as having the devious purpose to prove "I am" because "I was." Against these attempted ravages of present peace, the hour is our bulwark, an impregnable fortress in the many storms of the story of time. Here in the cathedral of light, we need ask for nothing, because, in the quietness of its sanctuary, we realize at last that the Answer we seek is, in truth, what we are.

THE FOURTH FLOOR, PART III

We should not underestimate the value of learning to live fully in the light of the present hour in a place, i.e., a time and space, with an ultimate significance—other than how it can be used for our awakening—on par with a sneeze. With sufficient faith in ourselves, living in the present and doing what feels right—by never doing what feels wrong—can become the outside expression of the inner conviction that we truly deserve to always be at peace. Peace of mind is the goal of every awakening light, for in the uncertainty of the game, no other support can be relied upon. It may seem strange to have worked for decades only to discover that what we have been searching for is in the hour that has always been, and is, in front of us. But not so strange once we realize that we were engaged in building up the necessary trust to get here. And now, at first, until it becomes completely natural, we need to practice the skill of remembering to remain here, reining ourselves in and returning every time we enter forgetting and go galloping off into the sunset of a past that is no more, or into the twilight sleep of a future that may never come to be.

Faith in ourselves as part of the Self, with the inherited right to live in peace in the hour, comes only with disbelief in the terrible tale that because bodies, or stories, have made mistakes and vary, anyone could be essentially different and better than anyone else. To believe that some of us were created superior to, or holier than, others, or that some have successfully used free will to improve themselves mightily, while others have failed miserably, or to buy into the idea that slower learners or the less competent deserve to be left behind, are despicable thoughts so hateful at the core, they don't belong in our minds. Comparisons and judgments are never based on objective standards, because once we begin to dance with these unworthy partners, we are no longer objective. Any scale that finds us greater than some will automatically declare us to be inferior to others. How, then, in such criticism-laced circumstances are we to find the comfort and rest that come only to those who learn to look beyond appearances, recognizing every light, or mind, as an equal and a friend?

Seeing beyond form, we begin to realize that the real function of stories, or bodies, is to act as instruments through which we, who are lights, can express our renewed state of mind. Only as our awakening gains traction can we accept Storyland as a classroom, and then free others to learn their lessons in the ways they so choose. An equal is an equal is an equal, with every equal an equal part of the Self, and therefore equally as worthy as another. Again, the truth we seek is not outside us but within, as we are within it, all else being a restless dream, an illusion, and a lie. This is the truth we will discover as our own when we share it with everyone who is or has ever been—or better, seemed to be.

While the reality of Storyland may be that few people are awake enough to care, that, however, is not the point. The point is we will know *we* are awake enough when we no longer care that they don't care. The simplicity of it all is that those the world calls "sinners" are really confused "saints," "saints" being no more than those who became wise enough to refuse to act on the evil thoughts that "sinners" still foolishly embrace.

If someone is slippery at the moment, that is just where he is at in his awakening, like every other Janus-faced self-tormentor unaware of the real source of his distress. His need is ours: to realize that associating with comparative or judgmental thoughts in our minds is like associating with criminals in the world. To refute these thoughts is to teach that peace is safe, learning at the same time the power of our minds to deny that any problem we have has us, all thinking to the contrary being most unbecoming to the lights, or minds, we truly are.

Developing the power of our minds also involves strengthening the conviction of our ability to overlook form, which means nothing. Instead, we must seek for content, which means everything, becoming aware that the perception of either guilt or innocence—the only two contents possible—*always* comes from a decision within, and *never*, from an event without. Nothing comes to us from the outside. If something from the outside, be it good or bad, "registers" with us and evokes a response, it is always because it has met its counterpart within. To give what appears to be evil a new interpretation and see it as a plea for understanding from a mind, or light, that doesn't understand is to understand what it means to disregard the importance of form by always giving precedence to content. We are here to help, not hinder, the progress of all, this being the way we make progress ourselves.

As darkness is the absence of light, and guilt the absence of forgiveness, so ignorance is the absence of adequate information, and actually nothing else. It is ignorance that causes confusion and makes people fearful, as it is fear that makes them hostile in turn. Once we understand this, we'll neither judge nor oppose, and in that, prove to ourselves that *we* are no longer ignorant and, consequently, no longer need to be fearful or hostile as we were. This is how our negative thoughts and their mean murmurs are found to be no more than the clang and harsh peals of a bell never rung.

If in reality the only "sin" is sleepiness, meaning that when people think unfairly or act wrongly, it is simply because they are not awake to what is right, *there is no sin.* Accepting this translates easily into the idea that people function poorly or well to the *exact* degree they are either ignorant or aware. Essentially, a nasty person is a frightened person, and a frightened person is an uncomprehending person, and an uncomprehending person is a pleading—for someone's understanding—person (read: mind), and so a pleading person is an unknowing person; therefore, a nasty person is really an innocent person (again, read: mind) in disguise.

If we, who have been at times victims of the nasty and at other times quite literally their victimizers—if in no other way than by our so-called "hurt" or our judgments—are willing to accept what *we* have been doing for what it is, we can find reason to say to our seeming opponents—past or present—two things that will set us free from our wrong-minded needs to accuse, attack, and blame:

1. "I am truly sorry that I tried to bring harm to you, be it in the situation in which I was acting as the victimizer or the one in which I was playing the victim, instead of laughing at the idea I was in need or could be placed in—mental—distress by anyone at all."

2. "In either case, thanks for going through that difficult episode with me. I didn't realize it at the time, but I now see what an aid it was in my reaching this place of a better understanding of what I was so confused about before: that no matter which role I appeared to be in back then, I am completely responsible for how I think and feel about both you and myself right now."

And then, because we *are* all the same, to greet the others, who, dead or alive, will be or are saying the same two things to us, with the following responses:

1. "It's nothing. You don't even have to say you're sorry, because through the process of reflection on our interaction and an honest examination of my old disoriented thinking, I've learned I was not and am not hurt in any way at all."

2. "You're welcome. I'm glad our interaction helped you as much as it helped me."

These steppingstones to true forgiveness are the ways we learn that *no one* is evil; that we've *all* been mistaken because we've *all* been ignorant; and how we reach the place of understanding that, in truth, *not one* of these past problems ever happened at all. To say we remain innocent is to say to all other, and our own, dreaming minds, "All thoughts of the violation of your eternal purity are untrue." This is equally to proclaim Storyland a falsely tragic and triumphant farce set in a fictional kingdom, the sole quality of which is deception surrounded by the dark clouds of a lie. In the denial of separation, the basis for guilt and guilt itself are rendered impotent, the doors of the cathedral opening wide in welcome to those we'd see as classmates and offer sanctuary to as like-minded friends.

The most difficult lesson is to learn to meet attack without attack, and the only non-fake way to do that is to understand the source of others' distress. Belligerence—hostility, dismissiveness, impatience, condescension, in-tractability, rudeness, and the like—on the part of the unfriendly, examined calmly, can be seen to have its source in fear, and fear recognized as no different than pain. To perceive fellow minds, or lights, as suffering in pain is to find just cause to refuse the temptation to meet their psychological slaps with "fists of fury" and, instead, extend the gentleness of our Self to those who feel alone and bereft.

This is not a pacifist statement that says to the unaware, "I'm so much better than most, please come and walk all over me." Rather it suggests that we live normally, doing what feels right—meaning again, not wrong—saying "yes," or "not now," or "no," as seems appropriate, remaining aware that what is *always* appropriate is to meet those who are in trouble with a compassion that touches their pain with hands made soft by our remembrance of the Truth.

It takes great determination to remain alert to the fact that when others betray our—often unseen—version of what they should be doing, they are not presenting us with an opportunity to pounce on them in "righteous" indignation, but a chance to not again betray the sacred trust we have with our Self and, therefore, with the mistake-maker as well. If we refuse to listen to the voice of reason that says, "Here's another opportunity to be kind, that you may remember you *are*, in reality, *only* kind," and instead spurn the rights of an equal in distress, we will once more have fallen into the trap of believing it is possible to separate our interests, and to find gain in what is clearly division and, so, loss.

This is the plight of everyone who believes in the fantastical fallacy and laughable lunacy that attack could *ever* be made in safety, and that what is forever One has been rendered asunder and divided into warring parts. This is the fearful fairytale every mind that believes it is a story, or a body, is suffering from unnecessarily, the terrible self-deception it must face in order to learn it is not so. No one gets healed of a pernicious mental illness through a process of denying he is ill. Nor is there anything outside his mind with the power to impede his healing the moment he sets out to do away with the disease of wanting to be different from those who, in truth, are equal parts of the Self.

What upholds the belief in our differences as meaningful is our taking them seriously. And what upholds the seriousness is the ugly fact that, in our desires to be special, we want the differences to be real, this hidden agenda being the unseen cornerstone of everyone's grief, fear, and pain. And yet, as we learned our way into this hornet's nest of guilt, so we can teach our way out, recognizing that no one finds the peace he or she seeks by categorizing differences, only by discovering they are unreal.

In a practical sense, this means that when we are tempted to be disturbed by what we see as an outside event, and choose against that self-deception, what disappears is not the person or the problem, but the misperception that the person or the problem had the power to dislodge us from the oasis of peace. In other words, disturbance comes not from the outside at all, only from seeing through a glass darkly and falling prey to the harsh barbarians of blame.

Since outside denial, or the unbelief, the negative of the positive does not exist, *all* charges made against us by the storyteller have been dismissed. Not on a technicality or a jury's whim, but on the solid grounds they were baseless because—other than in the fiction of duality—there never was an "us" for the charges to be leveled at. What this comes down to is that either the most grotesque sight in the world is an eerie apparition and our worst memories are blatant lies, or evil exists and Truth is not true because it is no longer all that is. Either the "I am" of great expectations and a seeming personal importance is no more than the storyteller's peculiar presentment in the great fable of a fall—again, the myth of a "fall" being necessary to the myth of "I am"—or we are real people in a real world, and all speculation to the contrary is just presumptuous nonsense and nothing else. Either these things we have conceived of as ourselves are no more than flickering falsities, developed out of the shadows of a lie, or everything we see is not only evident and tangible, but substantial and real. Either as lights, or minds, our only real problem is one of misidentification with an enfeebling fraud we invented and now think of as "me," or our serial adventures and misadventures in this world are quite serious and in no way fictional at all. Either *all* of time and space is an untrue story being told by an untrue story, a dream with no more lasting reality than the nightmare you or I had when we were nine, or what is changeless and one *can* change and become better and worse, and we're actually made of dust, and to dust we will return.

Bad things made seemingly real and kept in memory, although they are long gone and never were what they seemed, are simply ogre-ish tales of the storyteller meant to frighten our still-mistaken and confounded minds. The worst "crime" of our lives is there for us to look at, go through, and then smile back on in silence, this being the only lesson we can learn from a powerless thing. Yes, we have to say—and mean—"sorry" and "thank you." But only to learn through such unflinching responsibility that, in reality, our errors never happened at all. The utter madness of the game of "I'll show you, manipulate you, beat you, get you, blame you, seduce you, reject you, and, if necessary, destroy you in the process in order to get what I want" speaks only for duality as reality and, therefore, never of our Self or the Truth.

The unvarying, non-circumferential, and unlimited wholeness of Truth cannot be described, because there is no one apart to do the describing and nothing else to compare it to. It cannot be delineated, because it has no borders. It cannot be defined, because it is not specific. It cannot be apprehended, because thought, even at its highest levels, can never go beyond its own dualistic limitations. It cannot be approached, because there is nothing outside it. It cannot be conceived of, because there is no conceiver to have a conception of what can only be known. What, then, can be said of it in the vast entirety of the ever-changing universe of time and space? Because silence is the real answer, nothing at all.

How, then, are we to rest assured that the Truth is true, trustworthy, and beautiful beyond conception and measure, always welcoming and forever only perfectly benign? Simple. How else could our Self be? Judgmental, offended, harsh, critical, retributive, or the like? Those are just the mean-minded misunderstandings of caged thought given expression, hectoring foolishness pretending to make sense. The real understanding we seek comes from the greater understanding that because only Stillness means something, nothing else means anything, and so there is, in the calm of the Self, nothing to understand. And so, again, we come to that great seeming paradox of illusions: nothing to understand because there is no one to understand; no one to understand because there is nothing to understand. Who is there to understand this? No one. What is there to understand? Nothing.

The drawings—images, stories—we made of ourselves were writ not in ink, but pencil, and are as impermanent as we would have them be. And since we alone are the ones who drew them, shaded them, disapproved of and "improved" them, loved them, hated them, and fought with others about them, who but us can erase our attachments to what is variable and, therefore, impermanent and unreal? And *what else* would we want to do with them once we saw them for what they are?

The real meaning of our lives in the game is to learn that there is no meaning to our lives in the game, for the "people" of the game are the people of stories, not what we, as lights, or minds are at all. There is no real connection between our minds and our stories—only a hypnotic or dreamlike one—our earthly lives just an unfortunate aspect of our belief in a "fall from grace" and other sad stories about the macabre and unreal. Yet our minds retain the power of choice, so we can change our viewpoints and engrossments with the false, realizing that the only sane approach to peace is elimination of our investments in the so-called pleasures of conquest in the terribly cruel game.

In one sense, we might say that the many conflicts of the world—all the attacking of "those others" and the constant defending of personal interests—have as their purpose to prove both the storyteller and its concept of self are substantive and real. And while the storyteller's effectiveness at promulgating such tales of opposition and misery cannot be denied, the veracity of its interpretations can and must be. How else to escape from the excitement and despair we've given power to rule our minds but to deny all power to what denies the reality of Truth and the calm Wholeness of our Self?

We are where we are in the world of the game because that is the way our—seemingly karmic—stories of intermittent woe and satisfaction are spinning out, not because of a lack of concern, or the special favor, of some overarching power. Implied in the idea that there is something that finds us and singles us out for a blessing is the hidden thought that this same something at times loses sight of us and leaves us rotting in little better than a curse. How could there possibly be something above that goes, "Oops, I forgot you for a moment, but now that I've got time, let me give you a hand," other than in myths that accomplish little more than further frightening the already uncertain and confused? The problem with all this, including the wishful fairytale of finding "the Secret" or of using the "power of prayer" to compel attention, is that none of it appears insulting on the surface, because we don't recognize the accusation of carelessness it keeps hidden from sight.

We are not, as many have taught, the threatened victims of "original sin," put here to become worthy enough to be saved, or given an "it's up to you now" permission to misuse free will and be damned; to be run through the wringer now and maybe, if we are good, later patted on the head and set free. We are not pitiful "I ams" wandering in a shambles with little to hope for in all our travails except a future home in a heaven we are not even positive exists. Or, if it did exist and we arrived at its door in a Kafkaesque tale without sense, that we'd even be among the ones on the list to be invited in.

What, then, in all this "supposedness" does make sense? Accepting full responsibility for the story, or belief, that gives seeming reality to the storyteller's pseudo-existence; admitting our central role in the hopeless quest to pump the breath of life into stillborn stories of self animated by nothing more than hot air; setting aside our covetous desires to make our images grander than most through the contemptible means of comparison and condemnation; challenging our fears and, in that, uprooting the foundation of "the—guilty—me"; and, finally, realizing how impossible it is for there to be a "better" and "worse" in a reality that is One, or that there could really be a "we" to be judged and held responsible because of errors made in a fictional Storyland that was and is no more than an illusion to begin—and end—with.

Nothing can disturb the stillness of our unstained Reality, a Reality unmoved by dreams and incapable of change or of being in touch with anything but a Truth as eternally perfect as Itself. Forget the dissembling arguments of the "fighters against evil" in the unbelief who seek to convince us it is arrogant to conceive of ourselves as innocent, and humble to confess to being the miserable sinners they insist we must be and are. Instead, let us look carefully at the world this thought system based on separation and fear has produced. And, as we do, let us also remind ourselves of the power of discernment given us for the purpose of looking without concern on the distemper of chaos, with its help coming to the simple conclusion that what makes no sense *makes no sense.*

EPILOGUE

And now we come to the final stage of our journey through the metaphorical house: from the Dionysian bacchanalia of the cellar; through the levels of the cruel game of sabotage in the icy river; the beginnings of the understanding of true forgiveness as the retraction of projections, and an inner choice as the deciding factor in perception; the importance of constantly observing the mind's activities; our urgent need to refuse to continue to be swept away by the siren calls of fear that would have us bow down to the ugliness of guilt; and, finally the fourth floor's quiet recognition that since all the many facets of Storyland are changing and disappearing as well, *not one of them* can be worthy of more than a mild shrug of vanishing concern.

Every single person we seem to know, have known, or will come to know in Storyland, ourselves as we think we know ourselves included, is a story *we* are telling *ourselves*, each no more than an imaginary figure in our own untrue dream. Everything we believe is important, outside of learning this single lesson, is equally an aspect of what is literally fading away and so has no lasting meaning. If we were to put our case simply, in the deepest sense, it would go something like this:

What we do is *not* important

Because we are *not* important

Because *no one* is important

And *nothing* anyone does is important

Because Storyland is *not* important

And *nothing* that happens in Storyland is important

Because there is *no* Storyland

Because it is *all* made up

And therefore means *nothing* at all.

It is to the sanctuary of the cathedral of light of the present hour that everyone must return to rediscover his or her own power of choice. It is here we come to see that we've made weakness dominant and our strength submissive, learning to exercise that strength and scoff at illusions, reversing what we've mistakenly believed in as the reality of our plight. Our goodness is real and our potential is unlimited, but our faith in ourselves, really our trust in the Self, needs to be nourished in order to grow. And so we practice our lessons daily by saying "says who?" to bad memories and "we'll see" to worries about a future unknown, responding with the seven *n*'s ("no, no, no, no, no, no, no") to all thoughts of negativity that call us to follow them into the slough of despond, and with silence to whatever residue or echoes that follow in their wake.

Perhaps we have learned by now that our only *real* problem is believing we are the ones—the stories or bodies—with the problems, and that solving this problem while calmly dealing with all the others is the one way to set ourselves free. We cannot escape from a trap we are not in, but we can, and must, come to realize that what seems to be trapped cannot be ourselves, really our Self, whose very name means freedom itself. We *are* freedom, and as we remove our support from stories born of limitation, we can look on all the turmoil in this subversive world—up to and including that weird form of disappearance called death—with a rational mind that says, "How could such fraudulent witnesses to eternal Truth be anything but unreal?"

The process we are engaged in is one of correcting our having taken seriously the belief in a writ of divorce from our Self that could not and, therefore, did not happen; undoing the dualistic notion there is such a thing as a believer and something external or of a different quality to believe in. Because there is, in Truth, only the Self, or the One, all speculation about anything else must ultimately be the nonsense posing as sense. This makes the world of stories a greatly enlarged version of the Tower of Babel, a vast scene of clamor and confusion wherein *all* that takes place has no more significance than a vanishing puff of smoke.

When we finally realize that the world we seem to inhabit makes *no* sense, that things happen unexpectedly and unpredictably, and that we really have no way of figuring things out, the logical answer to such instability becomes living fully in the hour and letting the rest take care of itself. When our focus is truly in the present, we can better accept that we are here not primarily for personal gain, but to learn about our minds, because *everything* we see, hear, think, feel, believe, and remember comes from the way our minds work and from absolutely nowhere else. The alternative is to continue ponderously plodding in a dim-witted plundering of things that subtract from our character and add nothing to our peace of mind.

All this takes a while to accept because it requires abandoning a thought system based on the interests of self coming not only before those of others, but even before the care of our minds—many unaware there is such a thing. The difficulty in this is relinquishing a belief system we have built so carefully and religiously to defend the story of self that letting it go seems almost like relinquishing a loved one into the arms of death. And yet it is life, not death, to put away selfishness and hopes of specialness, and only foolery to cling to them as though they spelled safety for what is not. What is founded on the premise of our having rights inherent to ourselves and not equally to all others is attempted suffocation of the spirit and starvation of the soul. These are the Trojan horses accepted by unbalanced minds unaware of the enemy within and its intent to destroy.

And yet, what power can an inner delusion or an outer illusion really have? In truth, no matter what seems to be happening either in Storyland or in the realm of our misunderstanding wrong minds, everything that is real remains Perfect and changelessly as it is. Our Self knows nothing of Storyland, or of the many peculiar happenings and mad tales told here. No more will we when we awaken from this weird dream and remember to laugh at the disappearing dualistic deviousness we one and all took so seriously before. But first we must learn to appreciate *everyone's* struggles; overlook mistakes made in ignorance in an attitude of goodwill; and no longer insult equals and flatter our egos by assuming we are special in any way at all.

To make our way out of the conflict and grim confusion of Storyland and enter a world of non-opposition we barely could conceive of before is to

- Learn to live in each hour as though it were fresh, and solitary, and totally brand new

- Greet each person who enters with respect and as if we were meeting someone of importance for the very first time

- Treat the troubled and the untroubled alike, and as we ourselves would wish to be treated

- Trust the direction of our Self by doing or saying what feels right, or better, by *not* doing or saying what feels wrong

- Be willing to respect another's right to be wrong for as long as the fear of being otherwise remains dominant in his or her mind

- Recognize better that the grievances we have difficulty uprooting are difficult to uproot only because they serve so well as defenses of the self

- Not deny responsibility when we become impatient with the impatient or the unruly, as if our impatience was different or better than theirs

- Refuse to put on the mantle of "rescuers" of benighted souls supposedly lacking the blessing of minds as powerful as our own

- Deal calmly with whatever takes place, even when part of our thinking is jumping up and down

- Remain aware there is no answer to the lament of "why?"—only the realization that nothing remains unjust the moment we use it as a means to regain the remembrance that not one thing in Storyland is true

- Accept that all things—people, situations, events—are neutral until given meaning by our interpretations

- Perceive guilt as arrogance, not humility, because it proclaims us as "I ams" that are real, separate, and capable of harm

- Understand that when Storyland is finally perceived as a mirage, what disappears is not the mirage, but the belief it contains water, i.e., something of worth

- Stay in the center—outside time and space, thought and memory—where the strength of balance is. And when we become disturbed by the ephemeral, accept that it is because we've left that place of safety, and for *no other* reason at all

- Realize that no matter how much we hide it from awareness, we cannot condemn others without believing the same standards will be applied to ourselves

- Aim, with the help of a burgeoning fortitude, to remain quietly cheerful in the many tribulations of time because that, and not moroseness, is complementary to what we are

- Learn to say to what makes no sense, *this makes no sense*, instead of gullibly swallowing whole that choking nonsense "it's a mystery"

And, above all,

- Apply ourselves willingly not to the task of "self-realization," but to the removal of the ignorance that proclaims us as anything ever "unrealized" and apart from our Self.

It is in the cathedral alone we can breathe without the conjoined constriction of the twin terrors of guilt over what was impossible and fear of retribution from a stern judge who, outside our delirium, simply does not exist. And it is here as well, in this hour of true forgiveness, that death, when its time comes, can be greeted not as the great opponent to be fought against, but as a benevolent companion sent to guide us either back home or on to the next stage on our journey. And from this more rational reference point, we will look back not in anger at others or regret over our mistakes, but in gratitude for what they taught us and appreciation for all that we've learned.

We are *all* integral parts of a Self that alone Is, as holy, complete, and innocent as Oneness Itself. We *cannot be* disenfranchised, disavowed, forsaken, or judged, any more than it is possible we be reprimanded or punished; rather simply forever deemed worthy of the fullness and the tenderness and the goodness of Love. We are the Light beyond all shadows, the Song behind all notes, the Stillness that knows nothing of the disappearing noise, the perfection of Truth at the heart of the Absolute; never in reality an "I," a "you," or a "me"; only, and always, in essence the Magnificence that Is, one with the Wonder of Wonders—nothing else, nothing less, evermore.

ACKNOWLEDGMENTS

This book is dedicated to Dr. Kenneth Wapnick, the late president of The Foundation for *A Course in Miracles*, the wisest teacher and best friend a person could hope to have. My gratitude to him is matched only by my gratitude to my wife Kathy, which lessens in no way the gratitude I feel for Gloria, and every member of my family, deceased or alive, who each and all have helped me in ways too numerous to describe.

I'd also like to thank every friendly *and* unfriendly person I've ever met—the friendly ones for reminding me that the real goal of life is to always be kind; the unfriendly ones for teaching me that I need no friendship from another I cannot supply to myself.

Finally, I would like to thank Chris Zook for his excellence in editing, his helpful insights, and all his dedication and hard work in completing this manuscript and keeping it coherent.

Also by Robert E. Draper:

Silence Is the Answer ... to All the Noise of Doubt

"This is one of the few books I have read in the last several years that has touched me deeply, and I find myself going back to it often to reflect or to learn from its insights. Without reservation, I highly recommend this book."
    – Michael Pancer, Amazon.com Reviewer

"Robert Draper's personal journey and quotes from sages past and present make this book compelling and relevant. .... Completely unlike other 'self-help' books you've read."
    – Cara Gillette, Amazon.com Reviewer

"Silence Is the Answer—To All the Noise of Doubt is an extraordinary, well-written, profound book and one for the ages.   – Tom Brown, Amazon.com Reviewer

*The Other Side of Success ...
    And All Its Empty Promises*

"An inspirational look at one man's journey from meaningless success to a life of purpose."
    – *Kirkus Discoveries*

"The Other Side of Success is written from the perspective of a man who has learned hard lessons about life's challenges. In the end, Robert Draper does a superb job of sharing his wisdom and conveying hope."   – Barry Silverstein, *ForeWord Clarion*

"I recommend this valuable collection of insights to anyone who, in spite of following all of the popular advice on professional and personal success, still feels empty and is truly ready to try another path."
    – H. W. Beach, Amazon.com Reviewer

Available in print soft cover and eBook format at Amazon.com and other retail outlets.

9832310R00068

Made in the USA
San Bernardino, CA
28 March 2014